THE BEST OF JIM MURRAY

THE
BEST
OF
JIM
MURRAY

Doubleday & Company, Inc., Garden City, New York

796
Mur

1. Sports – Annecdotes,
facetiae, etc.
I. Title.

To my three sons, Ted, Tony, and Ricky, who have never read my columns and doubtless won't read this book, and my daughter, Pammy, who won't, either. To their mother, Gerry, who not only read, but, bless her, laughed at all the jokes.

Foreword

The only thing I know for sure about sports is that they need dramatizing.

This is perfectly apparent to the owners of professional sports teams. The first thing you need after you get a franchise is not a player but a press agent.

Walter O'Malley, who needs no introduction here, once said that the main reason he moved the Dodgers from Brooklyn to Bedlam-by-the-sea (otherwise known as Los Angeles) was because Brooklyn lost its only daily paper, the Brooklyn *Eagle*. "And anyone who thinks he can run baseball without a daily paper, can't run baseball," succinctly observed Walter.

This is not so apparent to athletes. "You guys live off us," Leo Cardenas, a not-otherwise so acute observer has stated. Leo was stating the case for a good many athletes who privately share the same notion.

The evidence is clear the opposite is true. Baseball and all other athletics rode an ascending curve into Big Business on a wave of news clippings that could re-forest the Northwest if they could be turned back into trees. And that's probably the only way they could begin to redeem the damage they've done.

Leo Cardenas, it might interest him to know, would probably be making one-fifth the salary he is making—if

that—if it weren't for the enormous (not to say unwar-
ranted) attention journalism pays to sports, particularly
baseball. And Leo might be earning it with a machete instead of a bat. Willie Mays has been known to demand
$500 for interviews from writers whose gratis encomiums
in the past have put Willie precisely in the position where
he is able to demand that kind of money.

Catching a fly ball, or hitting a curved one, is not all that
difficult. It may rank in degree of difficulty somewhere below juggling Indian clubs and above playing an ocarina.
Willie gets $100,000 a year for this relatively meager talent.
Diamond-cutting is infinitely more complex and difficult,
not to say useful, but diamond-cutters can't even get the
guy next to them on the bus to listen to them.

History shows athletics have been most successful on the
field and in the office safe (there is a 1-to-1 relationship
between the two, anyway) where the concentration of pub-
lications have been highest both in terms of quantity and
quality. It's not possible to measure what Baseball owes to
Ring Lardner, what Football is in debt to Grantland Rice,
or what Boxing owes to Dan Parker.

But it's possible to put a dollars-and-sense evaluation on
what Baseball, to take one example, owes to the Press
generically. Plenty. In the days before newspapers discovered the mutually advantageous benefits of huckstering
baseball as a circulation-builder, ballplayers made somewhat less than nervous pickpockets and somewhat more
than bricklayers.

Old-time ballplayers passed on a legacy of parsimonious-
ness. They were stingy because they *had* to be. Crowds
were fewer and their fame was not so widespread. When
their playing days were over, they didn't open a restaurant,
they took a job in the kitchen of one. Or, if they did open

one, the food had better be good. If Mickey Mantle opens one, all they ask is that he be there. No one cares what he eats if he eats it in the presence of a demi-god. And Mickey *is* a demi-god. Don't the papers say so? And the TV? And the cereal box? And the bubble-gum card? Doesn't everybody?

Which brings me to my point that, now that I have justified my calling, I will proceed to justify myself. It's not so easy. I have a writing style which leans heavily on what your old English Lit. professor would call "hyperbole." This is a two-bit word for "exaggeration" or exaggeration for effect.

I say Frank Howard "clanks" not to suggest you should put oil in him but to suggest some of the awesome massivity of this man. You can also note that he's so wide from wingtip to wingtip that he has to be licensed by the Federal Aviation Agency and that he can shake hands with the pitcher from home plate.

I try to entertain the reader and pique his interest. This, in turn, I have to think, might entice him to come out to the ball park and take a look at this creature. You can simply state the facts: Frank Howard is 6 ft. 7 in. and weighs 240. This is no fun. But suggesting his name should be *Frankenstein* Howard is.

Anyway, he does sort of clank . . .

Sportswriting, like any writing, is equal parts hard work, long observation and lively imagination. I can illustrate with the story of Casey Stengel. Casey Stengel is a white American male with a speech pattern that ranges somewhere between the sound a porpoise makes underwater and an Abyssinian rug merchant.

For years, sportswriters, after asking each other "Whadeesay?" would transpose this lively gibberish into English.

One day, a young writer from *Life* magazine was assigned to a feature on Ol' Case. He was almost in tears after a week. He had been shot down by this one-man language. He had a trunkful of notes but only a handful of verbs among them and some circumlocutions that met themselves coming back. He was told to take them to a trained writer, one of the best, Ernie Havemann. Havemann listened gravely while the cub read the tortured notes.

By the finish, Havemann's hair was standing on end. He couldn't believe his good luck. He knew a good thing when he heard it. Even if he couldn't understand it. "My God, does he *always* talk like that?" he exploded. "Get your hat! I want to get this wonderful man on paper!"

And thus, "Stengelese" was born. One man had the journalistic sense to spot the drama or the incongruity—what set this man *apart*. He put his finger on what made Casey exceptional. The rest of us have simply lived off it. So, in a sense, has Casey.

There are players who resent having the idiosyncrasy that makes them unique being spotted and exploited. There are reporters who wouldn't spot it if it was pointed out to them and who think "color" is wearing funny hats or having genuine nervous breakdowns or being generally boorish around the field. In such cases, I have to think Leo Cardenas' accusation "You live off us" is all too true.

In a larger sense, which I despair of ever making clear to him, Leo Cardenas is living off the talents of a long line of skilled storytellers. Baseball, as a game, is played everywhere. Baseball, as a game, prospers only in the big leagues. That's because it is imaginatively covered only in the big leagues. If Mickey Mantle and the New York Yankees dropped in, incognito and in disguise, on a sandlot game, a lot of people who stand up all night in a queue outside the World Series ticket office would hurry right past and, if someone said, "Who's that playing ball over in the park?" they would answer "Oh, just a bunch of guys."

The competition among writers for stories has perforce made athletic heroes household words. No one cares what you or I have for breakfast. But what Mickey Mantle has for breakfast moves on the A wire.

Again I say, I don't justify it. I merely say it exists. Journalism now has a stake in sports. But sports has its entire poke riding on Journalism. And when I say Journalism, I mean Television, Radio, the tie-ins, magazines, anything and everything, including subway cards, that participates in the conspiracy to make athletes seem larger than life and a far cut above mere jugglers, one-wheeled bicycle riders, trapeze acts, and streetcar conductors.

Readers always get you aside and ask you of an athlete "What is he *really* like?" You think about it a minute and you want to say, "To tell you the truth he's just a kind of average, moderately bright guy whom you'd find fairly ordinary except he does have this *one* talent—he can hit a thrown ball farther than any other man in the country right now."

Or, it may be, that he can run from first to second, or from the goal line to midfield, faster than anybody in the country right now. This makes people curious about him. This is where *your* job comes in. *You* have to keep them interested. First of all, you have to keep yourself interested. This isn't always easy, either. Boredom is the joker in the deck, the loose board at the top of the steps in the dark.

There's a story in every man. The challenge is to find it. Then the problem is to tell it without putting the customers asleep.

Hitting a curve ball is hard, Leo Cardenas. But so is this.

If I can say anything of myself, it is that I have *survived* three years of writing a daily column under this kind of compulsion. I have never found that Holy Grail of newspaperdom, the "column-that-writes-itself." That's like asking an overturned canoe to right itself.

The business is not easy. I do not commend the writing up ahead, I ask only that you know this: it did not "write itself." And I have the ulcer to prove it.

Contents

THE BEST OF JIM MURRAY

GENERAL

There Are Hardships

If you don't mind, I would like to say a word for those much-maligned knights of the press—the baseball writers. Since I have become one of them for the time, I take it very personally when people like that fellow in Kansas City award a baseball writer the "Poison Pen Award" and accuse him of trying to run his team out of town.

I mean, people like that just don't have any appreciation for what us truth-seekers go through on a road trip for the honor and glory of baseball.

For instance, you come into a city like Cincinnati at 3 o'clock in the morning. Now, if you have any sense, you don't want to be in Cincinnati at all. Even in daylight, it doesn't look like a city. It looks like it's in the midst of condemnation proceedings. If it was human, they'd bury it.

You have to think that when Dan'l Boone was fighting the Indians for this territory he didn't have Cincinnati in mind for it. I wouldn't arm-wrestle Frank Finch for it. To give you an idea, the guys were kidding on the bus coming in to Cincinnati one time and they decided that if war came, the Russians would by-pass the city because they'd think it had already been bombed and taken.

But Cincinnati isn't the worst hardship we have to go through. It's in the top ten, though.

You probably never thought about it but we have Blue

Laws, the truth squad the WCTU sends along behind us, and bartenders who put too much vermouth in the martinis —hardships that Dan'l Boone never dreamed about.

I have in mind a coat of arms for the baseball press, of whom I'm proud to be a member, a swizzle stick and an olive with a toothpick through it, rampant on a field of old expense accounts.

Consider the other torments: You have to get up by noon. You have to go to the ballpark at night and you miss all those good programs like "The Price Is Right" and the one where Polly Bergen puts on her glasses to be able to pick the real Wilt Chamberlain out of a crowd of dwarfs.

I even had to switch off "The Secret Storm" the other afternoon before I could find out whether that guy was cheating on his wife and whether he gave his secretary that mink coat because she hadn't made any mistakes—or because she'd made a lot of them.

But we journalists try to keep our spirits up. When you come into town at three in the morning this isn't easy. Unless you find the right bellhop.

One night in Philadelphia, some creep pulled a chair from under a baseball writer who was getting in shape to file his story in an after-hours joint. They took him to the police emergency hospital and his pals went with him to enjoy the surgery.

The only vehicle they had to take home was the paddy wagon. Some of them had made the trip before, under an arm lock, but this time as they drew up to the hotel, one of them tapped the driver on the shoulder to ask: "Do you mind letting us off around the corner? The players are bound to misunderstand this."

Well, you can see what a grind it is—especially since

baseball writers are at that awkward age. Too old for girls and too young for Lawrence Welk.

There was one celebrated baseball writer who held the listed league record for arson. He used to fall asleep smoking—and drinking, too, for that matter. He set so many hotel rooms afire that the insurance underwriters listed him just below oily rags as a major cause of fires in this country.

Smokey the Bear put out a special cartoon about him and the Fire Department canceled all leaves when he hit town. He didn't need a press card; he could be identified by the glare in the sky.

The fellows try to make the best of it. In a way that makes distillers happy, usually. But they also extract their revenge on the community they're trapped in.

Senator Griffin, the Dodger equipment manager, used to wait till he and a companion were about to step into a cab to head out of town when he would pause at the door and be overheard saying, "By the way, did *you* turn off the tub?"

The friend would look aghast, "I thought *you* did."

The Senator would shrug. "Doesn't matter," he would say airily, "by the time the water gets to the elevator shaft we'll be a hundred miles from here. Go ahead, driver!"

Meanwhile, back at the hotel, a four-bell alarm would go off, service would be suspended, guests would be interrupted at dozens of activities by frantic bellhops looking for a running bathtub.

Allan Roth gets even with a whole town at a time. He is interviewed in St. Louis on the Joe Garagiola radio show as "Irving Bleecker," the fan in the stands.

"What about that left-field screen in the Coliseum?" Joe asked him when that issue was hot.

"What screen?" asked Irving Bleecker.

"What do you think of Mantle and Maris?" Joe asked

him some years back. "Who?" demanded Irving Bleecker suspiciously.

"Mantle and Maris," shouted Garagiola. "Do you think they can hit enough homers to break Babe Ruth's record?" "Ruth was a pitcher," Irving told him flatly. "I know," shouted Joe. "But he turned outfielder." "Well," sighed Irving, "I wouldn't know about that. I only got as far as 1918 in the record book and from what I could see, I would say he was making a mistake. He could have been one of the greats."

You see? And you thought this job was easy.

Larynxes, Laterals

The writer, Bill Davidson, is mad at sportscasters. "The Big Mouths," he calls them in the title of an article in the current issue of *Show* magazine.

If the sportscasters return fire, this may touch off the most popular war since Hitler and Stalin. I don't know whether you know it or not, but basically sportswriters as a breed hate sportscasters as a breed. The reason is simple: Sportscasters make ten times as much money as sportswriters. Of course, so do ballplayers. But sportscasters don't have to hit the curve ball. In fact, they don't even have to recognize one if they don't want to.

The sportscasters, by and large, take a dim view of sportswriters, too. They don't make enough money and they drink too much. But Davidson is not writing out of personal pique. It so happens he was once a sportscaster himself. For Bill Stern, of all people. This was back in

1939–40 but the resultant damage to his psyche has not
healed yet.

Bill Stern has since had his troubles, but in the days
Davidson worked for him, he was riding high and loud.
He was known in the trade as "Lateral" Stern because he
lateraled off more running backs than Gino Marchetti.
Every time he miscalled a runner and his spotter frantically
corrected him with a wig-wag, he would call for a lateral
and at least end up in the end zone with the right ball
carrier.

Davidson faults Stern mostly, however, not for his bad
eye sight but for his good imagination. Stern could see
things that weren't happening 20/20. Like the time he described tenderly how Tommy Harmon was spending the
halftime of a football game cheering up his weeping teammate, Forest Evashevski. Evvy wasn't weeping. He was
trying to fix his underwear. When Davidson pointed this
out to Stern, Bill answered airily, "That's the reason you
make twenty-five a week and I make fifteen hundred."

A pretty devastating squelch, I would say. It taught
Davidson to be quiet even when Stern would take "perfectly logical little sports anecdotes" and give them a touch
of the cosmic like the time he came up with the tid-bit
that the Pope used to hear Frankie Frisch's confession
when he was at Fordham—Frisch, not the Pope. The Pope
never was at Fordham. And since Frisch never was at the
Vatican and couldn't speak any Italian except to cuss out
an umpire, the anecdote was a pure Stern-wheeler.

Stern's eyes really lit up, Davidson says, the time he
told him that Abraham Lincoln had dabbled a bit in
baseball and knew General Abner Doubleday. Stern took
that ball into the end zone by himself. As he told it, when
Lincoln lay dying, fatally shot by John Wilkes Booth, the

President sat up and called for Secretary of War Stanton, clutched his lapels and pleaded with his last words "Tell Abner Doubleday . . . don't let baseball die."

Lincoln, of course, did die. But Stern didn't even blush when he told that story, Davidson says. And, of course, who can deny that Doubleday—with a little help from Walter O'Malley—did keep baseball alive.

Stern was the best of the radio image-makers but not the first. That honor belongs to Graham McNamee who undoubtedly held the earliest listed world record for free-style fabrication. McNamee was the first guy in history to make a foul ball sound like a moon shot. A one-sided Yale-Army football game sounded like the climactic battle of World War III. The late Ring Lardner sat behind Mc-Namee at a Yankees-Pirates World Series game in 1927. "It was like attending a double-header," Lardner wrote in awe. "You saw one game and heard another."

The point was, McNamee's game was probably a lot livelier than the real one.

Davidson set a few guideposts for his adenoid artists. Nothing short of a tonsillectomy from the neck down is going to stop them, he fears. His requisites for his seal of bad practices include 1) Nonsilence. ("Talk incessantly . . . ten thousand words are better than one picture.") 2) Truth. ("Remember, truth is relative and should be used only to instruct. An error is never an error if your team made it. It is a sensational play on an impossible chance.") 3) Loyalty. ("You are to be loyal at all times to him who feeds you.")

A happy case in point of virtue No. 3, Davidson says, was Jimmy Powers, who used to report the Friday night fights not as they were but as they should have been. While a fighter was being systematically hacked to ribbons in the ring, Davidson recalls, "Jimmy Powers babbled away about the out-classed opponent's eight brothers and sisters at home and his vaunted recuperative powers"—none of which was visible on screen.

Then there was the tennis player who showed up with a hangover that only a brand-new drunk could cure. Davidson thought the public would be interested in the fact one of the players was trying to win the Davis Cup only because he thought it might be full of booze. "Kid," scolded Stern, "that man isn't drunk, he's exhausted. Don't you know a good story when you see one?"

That was Davidson's trouble. He did. So he quit the broadcasting business and stayed poor.

Dr. Joe and Bus

You may have already forgotten but I haven't. I refer to the fact the U.S. retained the America's Cup a while back on a display of superior seamanship in the waters off Newport, Rhode Island, once sailed only by Yankee sea captains and men named Morgan and Vanderbilt.

What gratified me was that the skipper, representing the snootiest yacht club in all America, if not the world, was Jewish—Emil (Bus) Mosbacher.

The reasons for my especial satisfaction are a bit complicated; so I will begin at the beginning.

It was seventeen years ago that our little baby, then only a year old, ran through the living room of our apartment, clutching a white elephant wedding gift we thought we had hidden away—a cream pitcher. He tripped. There was a sickening crash. His face was buried in the broken glass.

We were white-faced when we turned him over. And well we might have been. What had been a sweet little baby's mouth was now two gaping shreds of flesh. The blood was torrential.

It was the kind of accident that happens to every family but with our first-born we were frantic. The drive to the receiving hospital was a nightmare I can live over any time I want but I don't want to relive that one.

The next day, we brought him to our pediatrician, one of those stuffy popinjays the medical schools were turning out those war years at the taxpayers' expense and who looked at little children as just another impersonal battle-field dispensary case. "What were you doing with a cream pitcher?" was his first question. "My, you'll have quite a scar," was his next contribution to our peace of mind. I snatched the baby off the table and marched home before I strangled the doctor with his own stethoscope.

At home, I had no way to turn. Then the phone rang and my city editor, Jim Richardson, was on the phone. "Take him to Dr. Joe," he told me as if he were ordering me to cover a fire.

And that was how we met Dr. Joe, a saint in our house who saved a little boy's mouth and a mother's sanity. I won't go into the innumerable operations, or the time the baby ripped all the stitches out of his mouth and Dr. Joe personally carried him up the elevator, getting blood all over his suit and not minding, although Dr. Joe was a dapper man.

I do know what our whole family owes to Dr. Joe because my wife was pregnant with our second son at the time. I do know we could never pay him in money. For one thing, he wouldn't let us. When I insisted, he wrote a note:

"If my livelihood depended on the distraught parents of little boys who have had minor accidents, I would be a poor man, indeed."

"If I can ever do anything for you, Doc . . ." was all I could say. It seemed unlikely. But, one day, the phone rang, many years later.

Dr. Joe, you see, was Jewish. He had been born some place in Czechoslovakia, had studied in Vienna before he became the foremost plastic surgeon in Hollywood. He was a wise, patient man who loved the good things of life— good food, good drink, clothes which ran to the Beau Brummell. And he had bought a boat—a cabin cruiser, a kind of sea-going Cadillac of which he was very proud. Naturally, he bought the biggest one he could find, a yachting uniform to go with it, and he set out to find a mooring.

He was embarrassed when he called me. When I found out why, I was, too. "Jim," he said, "I hate to call you. But I want to join a club and I have been turned down twice and it is humiliating. Can you find one that doesn't think a Jew should remain on land? Preferably fenced off?"

You can imagine the hot shame I felt. When I thought of all the spoiled young jerks I had seen around the yacht anchorages or misbehaving in Ensenada, to deprive this great man of the simple pleasure of salt water camaraderie seemed a criminality beyond belief. The sea didn't care. The winds didn't care. Only man walks the earth in a cloak of his own fears. It makes him more dangerous than all the elements put together.

My wife knew something was wrong when I came home and asked what it was. "Bigotry has got its own Navy," I told her bitterly.

We got Joe in a club. That was 1958 and I believe it was the Corsair. For them, a bow.

Dr. Joe didn't battle the complicated world much longer after that. He took his own way out of life. So he didn't see the little boy grow tall and straight and handsome. If he were here, I'd call him up, and tell him. The boy won't even need a mustache, Joe. You can't see it any more. And you know who is the best sailor at the toniest club, Joe? A Jewish skipper.

Courting Lady Luck

I have at hand a letter from Dore Schary, the movie man who has gone straight and now puts plays on Broadway. In a reckless moment, I dismissed Dore once as "a Yankee fan." Personally, I would consider that grounds for a libel suit. But Dore wasn't even satisfied.

"I'm not 'a Yankee fan,'" he wrote. "I'm 'the Yankee fan.' Let me explain—better, let me illustrate: I will tell you how I helped Don Larsen pitch that 'perfecto' against the Dodgers in 1956. After watching the first two innings on TV I realized that I had brought Don along by sitting in the far corner of my couch with my right leg crossed over my left. Also, I had been holding my right hand against my right cheek. My left hand held a cigarette. Well, sir, for the rest of the game I sat there—my right leg over my left leg —my right hand against my right cheek—and each inning as the Dodgers came to bat I lit a fresh cigarette and held it in my left hand."

Dore, for risking St. Vitus's dance and lung cancer to bring Larsen home, likes to think of himself to this day as "the playing fan." Larsen is now an outfielder but Dore is still in a living-room crouch. He is not alone, of course. I recall a World Series once in which I was taking a hair out of my eye when Dick Bartell hit a home run which helped the Giants beat the Yankees, 6–1. I had my eye closed when it happened, so I kept it closed the rest of the game and would have kept it closed the rest of the Series if the Giants had gone on.

The next day it rained and I went around like the man in the Hathaway shirt. I dared not open my eye and jinx the Giants. If they had won four straight I fear I might have kept it closed all winter, or at least put a patch over it, but the Yankees opened both my eyes wide the next day when they won 18–4.

If fans like Schary think they're superstitious, they should get a load of the players. You can always tell a ball team on a winning streak. The locker room smells like a flophouse. Most ballplayers wouldn't think of changing an article of clothing while they're winning.

Baseball is alive with outfielders who step carefully over foul lines as they come in to the dugout. Red Schoendienst takes his glove off between pitches when his team is ahead. Jimmy Piersall carefully marks out an "X" in the batter's box before he steps in. Eddie Collins used to keep a wad of gum on the bottom of his cap and whenever he got two strikes on him he would reach up, take it down and chew it.

Hairpins used to mean base hits and a batter in a slump would prowl the stands on Ladies Day in the days before women started getting crewcuts.

There are some ballplayers who don't hold with superstition. Like Zeke Bonura of the old Chicago White Sox. Les Mawhinney recalls Zeke used to drive to Chicago from his native New Orleans via New York and a friend once inquired whether this was for good luck's sake. Bonura shook his head. "I don't know how to get to Chicago from New Orleans," he explained. "But I know how to get there from New York. And I know how to get to New York."

When Zeke joined the White Sox, he had a well-earned reputation for thrift. Therefore, when he won the first game he played in with a late-inning home run, it pained him somewhat when his teammates advised him it was up to him to buy the beer for the whole team. Zeke didn't even believe in buying beer for himself but he had to give in.

As it happened, the team went on a winning streak. Each night, the superstitious players insisted Zeke stand drinks all around because failure to do so would jeopardize the winning streak. Zeke wasn't a bit superstitious—particularly when it came to his money—but he unhappily went along.

Finally, the day came when the Sox' great Ted Lyons pitched a heartbreaker but broke the streak, losing by one run in extra innings. Lyons was a hard loser and the clubhouse was a gloomy place as Ted sat there with smoke coming out of his nose, cursing mankind in general. The door burst open and in came Zeke Bonura—all smiles, whistling and humming, practically clicking his heels. "Well," he observed cheerfully, "you can't win 'em all." It was obvious he was mentally thinking, "Thank God" and it took the whole team to restrain Lyons from tearing his throat open.

Lefty O'Doul's superstition was the most famous. He wore a green suit for luck. It didn't always bring it. Harold Rosenthal writes of the time an imposter picked up a green suit and went around San Francisco representing himself as Lefty O'Doul, signing checks, running up bills, living it up. O'Doul was contacted, and disowned the man.

"Lissen," he said, "the next time a man in a green suit comes around and says he's Lefty O'Doul, take a bat and hit a fly ball to him. If he catches it, call the cops."

It's That Time Now

Elsewhere in the country, people didn't know the baseball season was on till Don Drysdale conked his first batter, Gene Freese broke the first ankle or Frank Howard missed the first outside curve ball.

But out in Malibu, I found out about it when I saw the little notice in the throwaway paper, "Little League Tryouts Saturday."

I tried to hide the paper but I wasn't quick enough. "Oh, boy. Little League!" the little one shouted. I couldn't have cringed more if I had heard "There's a skunk in the house."

You see, I've been through Little League with the two older boys. They're not getting any starry-eyed rookie in me. I know what Little League is—a juvenile activity that makes delinquents out of adults.

It's good for the kids, encourages skills, keeps them from hurting their eyes reading or helping around the house. It's the parents who come unhinged.

There are certain things you have to know before you start in Little League. When the fellow comes around innocently and says "We're looking for umpires this year," for heaven's sakes, if you have a business in town or if you're even around during daylight, say, "Not me, I don't know a Texas Leaguer from an Oklahoman."

If your wife belongs to any neighborhood clubs, it's best not to become a manager either. At the next club meeting, that redhead down the next block is sure to lean over to her and say, "Honey, why doesn't Jim play our little Donnie more? Is it just because Phil's dad is his boss?"

Unless you like to get cricks in your neck or cramps in your hand, don't be an official scorer either, as I was for three years. Little League is the citadel of no-hit 25–11 games. I think the record number for bases-on-balls was 108 in a double-header once. Of course, these were second-line pitchers. Front-line pitchers rarely give over 50 walks a game. Usually it's only about 48. This never encourages the umpires to shrink the strike zone. They learn how to umpire by the book in Little League. And the guy who wrote the book never saw a hard-ball game, either. I have seen infield-fly-rule arguments that I thought were going all the way to the Supreme Court—or the United Nations. Common sense has nothing to do with a manager with a wild look in his eyes and a rule book in his hand.

Then, too, there is the sweet young thing who comes up with eyes brimming and says "You didn't give Dickie an error on that last play, did you?" Of course, you didn't, you assure her, erasing furiously. Dickie only let a ball go through his legs, then whirled and threw it wild, clearing the bases. You look at those soulful blue eyes, the blond hair and the Capri pants that are just a trifle, thanks be, too tight and you think "What the hell, they're only kids. Can't expect them to play it like Jim Gilliam."

In our Little League, there is always a celebrity's son on each team. His father is the producer of *Bullsmoke* or *Frontier Moron* or something. Junior can't play very well but there's always the off-chance the old man will get Rita Hayworth or somebody to say a few words at the annual banquet about the proper role of athletics in everyday life.

Everyone was light-hearted at the tryouts. It was hard to believe, watching them all chatting together and mur-

muring, "You must come over," that, by mid-season, these same people wouldn't be speaking to each other and would storm off the field shouting, "Politics! That's all it is. Politics! You guys have picked on my kid for the last time!" Then, there will be the father who will stand there with a sick smile pretending he doesn't care as his kid is called out on strikes or thrown out at first. But that night, he'll shake the kid till he cries and yell, "Next time you get a bat on the ball, ya dummy, don't just stand there and look surprised. Run!"

You always take the kids to a Dodger game in the middle of the year. To See-How-the-Pros-Do-It. The night you take them, of course, is the night Snider, Neal, and Hodges bump into each other under an easy fly, the night Koufax can't find the plate, and Roseboro can't find the ball. And the public address system isn't working. The kids go home enormously encouraged.

You can see why I piled the little guy in the car with sinking heart. There's one hope: He's only 9 and might not make it. But in the tryouts, he crossed me up. He didn't catch the fly ball on the critical play. He was off at the crack of the bat. Unfortunately, in the wrong direction. The ball was going the other way. He slammed on the brakes, wheeled and lunged for the ball. But he's a natural-born ballplayer. Because when he saw he couldn't catch the ball, he fell down. Any dunce knows this is the right play in that situation. You not only don't draw an error, you draw sympathy.

Ricky, I'm afraid, is ready. I can see the Realty Board and the Mayfair Market fighting over him already. But the Mayfair will probably lose and have to take him. He's ready. His mother's ready (she's sticking pins in a doll marked "umpire"). The question is, am I?

A Letter from Jail

VERO BEACH—Letter from a man out of touch with civilization:

Somewhere in Florida.

Sometime in March.

Dear Honey:

Remember me? You know. The fellow who comes in for a change of shirts every so often and scares the kids? Yeah, *that one.*

Well, this time I really did it. If you get this letter it's because the currents are running west because I just dropped it in a bottle and tossed it through the bars into the Atlantic Ocean.

I now know what the prisoner of Shark Island felt like. You see, I'm down here at Dodgertown. That's a fancy name for Andersonville.

I won't say I was shook up when they showed me in here but I told them all I would do was give my name, rank and serial number. I didn't mind my room so much until I saw the sign on the wall: "This room has been redecorated," it said. That really depressed me. I mean—redecorated with tarpaper? The only hope was I looked down at the bottom to see if the notice had been signed by Nathan Bedford Forrest.

I know you told me to be nice on this trip and Lord knows I tried. Oh, I did ask the guy who showed us to our rooms if we got our mail through the Red Cross and said I supposed the trusties got slightly better quarters.

They tell me this place used to be a barracks for the

Navy. Up till now, I didn't know the Confederacy had a navy. The thing I really can't understand is why Sherman didn't burn this place down, too, while he was at it. He must have figured things were tough enough the way it was. It's not true, though, that he was looking at the Vero barracks when he got off his famous crack "War Is Hell."

The Dodgers train here because Walter O'Malley gets the facilities for $1 a year. It's the worst case of rent gouging I ever heard of.

The decor shows what can be done with plywood and a blank mind. There are no rugs on the floor. In parts, there's no floor. But it's a great place to train ball players. Or wild animals, for that matter. At night, there's nothing to do but sit around and listen to the plumbing drip. I tried to trace the leak and finally found it. The "I" had a hole in it in the "Made in the Confederate States of America" sign on the pipe.

I won't say the water tastes funny. But you do wonder whose swimming pool they pumped it out of. Either that or I would like to have as bartender the guy who poured the chlorine in. At least, I *hope* it's chlorine.

A word about Florida: It's as flat as a barber shop quartet after midnight. It's surrounded by salt water and covered by fresh air. It's a great place if you're a mosquito. An *old* Mosquito. Also white, of course. It was founded by a guy looking for the Fountain of Youth although what made him think it was here, I'll never know because Florida is full of old people.

I do have an upset for you, though. I *like* Vero Beach. It's a nice little old town. I think it was an air stop for the underground railroad. At night you can see the stars dancing in a thousand streams and smell the fragrance of a thousand orange groves. Or maybe it's vice versa. I forget.

But the Dodgers like it because they like a nice quiet town where they can keep their eyes on the guys after dark. Vero is ideal because any people downtown after 11 o'clock at night would go around bumping into light poles or each other.

It's a manager's kind of town. You know Walt Alston. The only guy in the game who could look Billy Graham right in the eye without blushing, who would order corn on the cob in a Paris restaurant. Walt doesn't hold with strong spirits or fast living. He always reminds me of Charley Weaver's uncle. You know, the one who bought the Pierce-Arrow with the window between the front and back to keep the sheep from licking the back of his neck.

Walt worries about me because he thinks I don't know enough about baseball—as if that had anything to do with sportswriting. Of course, he has reason to be nervous this year. All he has to do is win the National League pennant and the World Series. Either that, or he'll be showing people to their seats at Vero next year.

The Dodgers are in about the same condition they were last year. Some new phenom is on second base but they keep Jim Gilliam's shoes shined and spikes sharpened all the same. They're still hoping Frank Howard will break Babe Ruth's record and are now teaching him the two-handed swing to that end.

They are playing the Phillies as this is written. The Phillies are a team that has finished in the cellar four years in a row but this year they've made it tough on them by expanding the league to put what amounts to two other Phillies teams in it. The Phillies are going to have to concentrate to set a new modern record for low ball baseball. My money is on them, though. They have the stuff for it.

A guy who would write about the Phils would chop holes

in a lifeboat during a sinking, so I will only tell you what Jim Brosnan said. Noting that the Phils had a lot of guys on it named "Smith," Jim allowed that wasn't their real name. They were just trying to keep it from their families what they did for a living.

Love;

The man in Cellblock 7.

Akron of the West

I would appreciate it if you wouldn't breathe a word of what I'm about to say to San Francisco columnist Herb Caen. But *Sports Illustrated* magazine has put the knock on, of all places—hold your breath—*San Francisco!*

Personally, I couldn't be more shocked if the mag had called it Frisco. But they throw open the pages to a guy named Joe David Brown and the things he says about San Francisco shouldn't happen to Cincinnati.

It is a city, he says, which, in order, is—

Not as pretty as Asheville or Villefranche, wherever they are.

Just Akron with an ocean view.

Not a big league town.

Full of drunks.

A citadel of intolerance.

Vulgar and cheap.

It is, he claims, "not the lovely lady I had imagined but a vulgar old bawd . . ."

Even its restaurants he dismisses, with few exceptions, as "ptomaine parlors." It is a city alive with "goatish humor" and a "blaring forth of sentimental songs." It is a "Disneyland for drunks."

He goes on. Market Street is "the hardened artery of the West." Fisherman's Wharf is "only Market Street on the half shell."

The biggest tourist attraction is Alcatraz, he says. "San Francisco is a sick city, there's no doubt about it," he quotes a Health Department doctor.

"Never," sneers Brown, "have I seen so much sheer bad taste per square foot."

He marks the city lousy because it even booed Willie Mays. When Willie McCovey dropped below .300, he heard taunts "that couldn't be used in *Tropic of Cancer*."

It is a city, he suggests, that was "born to lose." Even the Beatniks are fakes. It leads the nation in suicides, mental disease, alcoholism. Cirrhosis of the liver is as common as the cold.

By last count, 244 people have jumped off the Golden Gate Bridge and all of them jump seaward at eighty miles an hour but get washed back to San Francisco in spite of the fact they chose to die with their backs to it.

A curious document, Mr. Brown's. Even the earthquake was second-rate, he says. "It wasn't even in the top dozen in the record books," he sneers.

What bemuses me about the article is this is the first person I have ever encountered around the sports beat who didn't like San Francisco. The sourest sportswriters on the circuit get lyrical when it comes to San Francisco. "The Paris of the West," was coined by a newsman. They put the knock on the wind at Candlestick Park, grouse about the press box at Kezar, criticize the parking. But they love The City.

Some of what Brown senses strikes a nerve, though. San

Francisco, as a city, has always seemed faintly overcivilized
to me, a place where, on certain occasions, you could feel
underdressed in a tuxedo.

San Francisco became the westernmost capital for goof-
ball zealotry like Zen, which one of its devotees once struggled to define by saying it could be explained as "the sound
of one-hand clapping." This offends Brown.

But he might be right when he says it is a city which
subconsciously does not want to win. Athletically, San
Francisco best exemplifies the old British tenet "No gentleman ever plays a game too well." Cases in point are the
Giants, the 49ers, Stanford, Cal.

When the Giants came to town and almost before they
had shaken the confetti from their hair in the welcoming
parade, the resident Beatnik poet got almost as much space
in the papers as the Opening Day pitcher when he wrote
the team was "a band of strangers who have nothing better
to do than hit a little ball around land that could be used
for far better purposes."

He acknowledged "there is a certain amount of poetry
in baseball . . . a player moves with grace and more people
should play it." But then he socked it over the head in
iambic pentameter when he added, "Watching it in an
expensive stadium where huge quantities of indigestible
hot dogs and soda pop are consumed helps nobody but the
promoters."

When Admiral Perry opened Japan, its troubles only
began. When Horace Stonham absconded with the Giants,
he opened up San Francisco and the East began to look up
the suicide rate, the fog, the accident rate. But, hang on,
San Francisco. Wait'll I tell you about Newark. *There's*
a big league city.

San Francisco is not so much a city as a state of mind. It has probably the only citizen in the world who would go right on eating crab and talking about art if the news came The Bomb was on its way. San Francisco, you have to say, has savoir-faire. Too much of it, in fact.

It is colder in the summer than it is in winter, consequently, you can recognize baseball fans by their chattering teeth, and football fans by their Bermuda shorts. It is a city which cannot make up its mind at night whether to go to the opera or the hungry i. No one wears shirt sleeves in San Francisco. In the first place, you'd shiver, in the second place, people would stare.

To give you an idea, San Francisco in the late 1800s used to have a character abroad in the streets who called himself "Emperor Norton I." He went around (and you could set your clock by him) in a uniform the Kaiser would have considered outlandish. He believed he was king and San Francisco let him. Anywhere else, they would have got a net over him but San Francisco permitted him to "levy" taxes, dine free in the best restaurants, and go his harmless way. It was hard to tell who was the biggest lunatic, he or San Francisco. He was terribly disappointed not to be assassinated.

The city hit a slump when he died. It might have been abandoned out of boredom if it weren't for the earthquake, which San Francisco characteristically ignored and grandly titled "The Fire," for the conflagration which followed, in the neatest bit of substituting effect for cause since the guy who killed both his parents pleaded for mercy on the ground he was an orphan.

But in 1958, things began to look up for San Francisco

again and everybody sat up, alert for the fun. The New York Giants came to town. The city was overjoyed. Twenty-five Emperor Nortons in baseball suits!

The Giants were just perfect for San Francisco, a faintly dotty band of athletes who had the good taste not to play the game too well. Of course, they had one super-player in the lineup, that fellow in centerfield, but San Francisco rejected Willie Mays' virtuosity as a bit vulgar. He seemed somehow to be missing the point.

But the rest of the Giants didn't. San Francisco was rocked for a while as the Giants soared into contention for the league lead each year. But the Giants nearly always caught themselves in time. So did the rest of the league. You couldn't set your watch by them, but you could set your calendar. In the hungry i, they would play the bit as follows: a business executive is standing in his office looking down over the city and dictating to his secretary. Suddenly, a falling figure shoots past the window. "Oh, oh," the man says, glancing at his chronometer. "It must be June. There go the Giants."

They built a new ballpark and the comedy got funnier. They went unerringly to the worst place in the city, if not the world, for it. Only the sides of Mount Everest could have been more unsuitable. The Giants became the only team in the game who played all their home contests in the teeth of a gale. A batter hit a ball, then ducked so it wouldn't bean him on the way back. The slopes of Candlestick claimed so many climbers whose hearts gave out that they were thinking of having St. Bernards roaming the moraines of the parking lot.

The Giants hired a house detective as manager and the city's applause was deafening. The evidence was the Giants needed a house dick all right. But not on the field. This was what is known in the trade as a "fire escape team."

Clancy Sheehan gave up, rumor has it because the Giants switched fingerprints on him. The management hired a tithing church-goer. The city feared the worst. San Francisco wanted a pixie not a preacher. Alvin Dark was a man who didn't drink or smoke and was as out of place in San Francisco as a bikini. Plainly, he could be expected to put an improper emphasis on victory.

The town needn't have worried. Alvin may not have had any bad habits but the team took up the slack. Almost his first official act was to bail out a considerable part of his starting lineup several hours past his bedtime, but several hours before theirs.

It was when he put Orlando Cepeda in left field that the city really relaxed. They would be subjected to no emotional binges like the World Series, after all, because the move made Orlando very unhappy and the facts of the matter were Orlando couldn't play left field even when he was happy.

Not only this, but the San Franciscan has insurance against victory better than any Lloyd's can give him. Anytime the Giants let him down, a disappointed San Francisco fan can always turn to the 49ers as the last best hope to uphold the tradition of the late Norton I.

Good-by to a Friend

This is a maverick in this book in that it's not a sports piece. It's a tribute, if you'll bear with me, to an old friend —the *Los Angeles Examiner*.

Los Angeles was a wildly exciting place when I first

went to work for the *Examiner* in 1944. The shipyards
were humming at the harbor, there were troop movements
going to every point of the compass, there were so many
murders the city was running neck-and-neck with the South
Pacific. Life was the only thing the OPA couldn't keep the
lid on. Life and Los Angeles.

There was seldom a dull moment. And if there were, the
front page of the *Examiner* never admitted it. Its shrill
calamitous presence was felt from Lincoln Heights jail to
the hibiscus-studded mansions in Beverly Hills. As young
reporters were in short supply that war year, we slept with
our socks on like firemen waiting for that next alarm in that
kookie city out there that made my native Connecticut
look like a monastery with a State House.

I fell in love with Los Angeles then, an affair of the heart
that I doubt I will ever outgrow and it was the *Examiner*
that brought us together. I never wrote sports in those days
but I never missed a sporting event either. I used to jeer at
the old Angels and bawl out a poor hard-working catcher
named Mickey Kreitner ("Kreitner, you're a bum!"). I
cheered the old Hollywood Stars where my favorite player
was a first baseman named "Butch" Moran because I ap-
proved of ballplayers named "Butch" automatically.

But most of my fun was in the city room of the *Examiner*. There was no such thing as a small story to us. We
lived at headlong apoplexy—from journalism school grad-
uates to gold-bricking old-timers. Our leader, hardly be-
loved, was a city editor who was such a combination of
literary light and Attila the Hun that his rewrite man,
Hank Sutherland, once dubbed Jim Richardson "Half-Oaf,
Half Elf."

The prose justified the dripping red headlines. When
Tokyo fell, there was almost nothing left but to sell a front

page actually in flames. Bodies were being delivered in
trunks to Union Station so regularly that we were thinking
of suggesting the railroad give special rates for them. Hollywood was alive with lurid stories. Louise Peete, who had
murdered one man, went to prison for half a lifetime, got
out and murdered again, sent the makeup editor trumpet-
ing through the city room, cackling "Louise Peete is in a
rut!"

So, I guess, were we. But we thought we were the luck-
iest guys on earth. New Year's Eve 365 days a year. On a
big story, the city room looked like a bust-out in an insane
asylum. Sob sisters turned out drivel by the ream, reporters dug up bloody angles by the edition. Murderers were
on the phone every other midnight, it seemed. The torso
of a young lady on an empty lot was enough to push the
steel strike back in the want ads as we set about to helping
the police solve the case. Neither of us ever did.

We had campaigns and sacred cows. The "Chief," Mr.
Hearst himself, was alive in those days and called at midnight almost as often as the murderers. Usually, he would
just want something like a croup kettle or an out-of-
manufacture cookie from his youth but he would periodically discover our city was in the midst of a crime wave—
usually when some acquaintance of the royal family got hit
over the head coming out of a night club—and we would
print a daily box score of crime, everything from spitting
on the sidewalk to double-parking. It scared hell out of the
tourists and we quit it.

There were heartaches, too. I remember almost the first
story I covered—a little girl on the north side got run over
by a truck and lost her leg. The thought of her going
through life that way made me shrink. It still does. She
must be twenty-one years old now and I wonder how she

has managed. I remember I had $8 left of my paycheck (which was only $38 to begin with in those days) and I bought her a whole armful of toys and brought them to the hospital and those silly nurses were embarrassed and told me I'd have to take them back, and I said, like hell I would, give them to that little girl or I'll bring the power of the press (whatever that was) down on you.

I don't know what they did with those toys any more than I know what life has done to that little girl.

I suppose the *Examiner* really died when the Old Man did. Newspapers, like other institutions, are lengthened shadows of men who love them and drive them. All I know is it died in its sleep. And part of all of us did with it. I hope I haven't bored you. But I just wanted to say good-by to an old friend.

History and Humbug

History, as someone once said, is humbug.

I mean, you probably think George Washington really did throw a silver dollar across the Rappahannock but it's highly doubtful. For one thing, he was too tight. Those who know him best say he wouldn't throw a penny across a bathtub without he had a string on it.

In the same vein, I think it was Jack Douglas who pointed out that at Bunker Hill the captain never said "Don't shoot till you see the whites of their eyes." What he said was, "If it moves, salute it. If it doesn't move, paint it. And if its eyes are white, shoot it!"

It's the same with sports history. It gets all distorted in

the re-telling. So what I'd like to do today is distort it some more—give you Murray's Mad History or sports as seen through a horn-rimmed monocle with a hole in it.

For instance, you undoubtedly think Babe Ruth was pointing to the bleachers for a home run he was about to hit that day in Chicago in 1932. Wrong. The umpire had just asked him where the gent's room was.

And Fred Merkle didn't forget to touch second base. He saw his teammates leaving the field and he suddenly remembered he had left his wallet on top of his locker.

Sports quotes are all fouled up, too. Here is the true story behind most of them:

"Say it isn't so, Joe." Now, this was supposed to have been uttered by a heart-broken urchin as Shoeless Joe Jackson came out of the courtroom after copping out to throwing a World Series. Actually, it was said by the doorman to Joe DiMaggio's apartment house the night the papers announced Joe and Marilyn Monroe were splitting up.

"Is Brooklyn Still in The League?" This was attributed to a sneer Giant Manager Bill Terry made in 1934, a piece of contempt that was to cost him the pennant. In actuality, this question was asked by a monk from Siberia who returned to this country after an absence of thirty years and took a subway out to Ebbets Field last summer. When last seen this monk was studying a road map to Chavez Ravine with a hurt look on his face.

"Win One for the Old Gipper." You all know the derivation of this. George Gipp, the great Notre Dame halfback, lay dying and called coach Knute Rockne down to him and gasped, "Coach, some time when the team is down and they don't have much chance and the Army is too strong for them, ask them to go out and win one for

the old Gipper." All this, of course, was according to
Rockne who had to wait several years till Army got strong
enough for him to need the quote. What history doesn't
tell is there was a Terre Haute gambler named Ambrose
the Gyp who also pulled Rockne down to his bedside one
night and said "Coach, some time when the team is down
and they don't have much of a chance and the Army is too
strong for them, take this ten-spot and bet it on Army and
win one for the old Gypper."

"Nice Guys Finish Last." This line is commonly pinned
on Leo Durocher who was on record as saying that unless
you would kick your grandmother's upper plate out to
score a run, you didn't belong in baseball. He was right on
that count. You belonged in jail. But the original use of the
quote dates back to a debate in the jockeys' room at a
famous racetrack one afternoon when the boys were trying
to set up the card that day to please everybody. But since
it was muddy, several of the guys said they didn't want to
finish last because they got sick and tired of changing
goggles. Finally, the ringleader got exasperated and asked
"Isn't there anybody here nice enough to finish last?" And
one guy stood up with a sigh and said "Well, if no one else
will, I will." And that's how the expression "Nice guys finish last" got started. Only they left out part of the quote.
The rest of it goes "on muddy days."

"Hit 'Em Where They Ain't" was supposed to refer to
Wee Willie Keeler who prided himself on placing banjo
hits where nobody could play them. Actually, the modern
usage refers to Frank Howard and the prizefighter, Pete
Rademacher, both of whom have long since eclipsed Wee
Willie's records.

"Baby, I Zigged When I Should Have Zagged" was what
Jack Dempsey was supposed to have said to his wife, Es-

telle Taylor, when he came home all beat up from the first Tunney fight. Actually, though, it's a direct quote from Wilt Chamberlain the night he didn't show up for the game and the coach went looking for him and found him stuck in a compact car.

"He Can Run But He Can't Hide" is what Joe Louis had to say about Billy Conn before their second fight but the truth is, the first time the quote was used was by the New York Police Department referring to Judge Crater.

Well, you can see how it goes, all down the line. You may even think "The Indians Are In-and-Outers" was first used by a Cleveland sportswriter but the fact of the matter is General Custer used it years before. "It's Not Whether You Won Or Lost, But How You Played the Game" also referred to General Custer and not the Rose Bowl and the West Coast as commonly supposed.

You'll never find any of this in history books. And that's not all bad.

A Root for Home

The only trouble with Spokane, Washington, as a city is that there's nothing to do there after 10 o'clock. In the morning.

But it's a nice place to go for breakfast.

I had really intended to quit the habit of knocking cities. Hang up my guns and go straight, as it were. But they wouldn't let me.

A delegation of leading citizens met me when I arrived in Spokane. After I ascertained none of them had a rope I asked what I could do for them. "Knock Spokane!" they yelled.

I saw my reputation had preceded me. I felt like the old gunfighter who gets challenged by a punk kid in each cow town he hits. "I can't," I told them desperately. "I've gone legit. Leave me alone, will you, I want to concentrate on writing sports."

"Listen," said one of them, clutching my lapels. "You can say it's the biggest collection of used brick in the world. They ought to knock it down and ship it to North Hollywood for fireplaces. How's that?"

I was panicky. "Terrible," I told him. "The Chamber of Commerce is bound to misunderstand. Tell me, you are a sportswriter, how will the Spokane Indians do this year?"

He ignored me. "You can say that on Saturday night there's nothing to do but go down and watch the trains come in," he went on, an unholy light coming into his eyes.

"But I've never been here on Saturday night!" I protested. "Who cares?" he persisted. "I've been here so many Saturday nights it makes me sick. And it happens to be true. There is nothing to do but watch the trains come in."

I made one last try. "I can't do it," I told them. "Besides, from what I can see Spokane is a nice little city." "But you're seeing it at an advantage," they cried. "It's covered with snow."

I tried a counter-attack. "What are you guys? Some kind of nuts?" I asked. "Don't you know there are 100,000 people who will leap to the defense of Spokane and call me all kinds of jerk? Why don't you knock the city yourself?"

"We can't!" they chorused. "We're in the middle of an urban renewal program. They ought to call it rural renewal. You're our only hope."

"But Bing Crosby came from here," I countered. "If he

gets sore he's liable to buy up the country and get me deported. You can't ask me to do this."

I shook free and went to the hockey game. They were disappointed but they followed me. On the ice, they were arranging a cardboard cut-out of a clown with a hole between his feet. "Put the puck in the hole and win a free car-wash," the announcer said.

"See!" my friends cried. "Did you ever in your life see anything more bush?" "I think it's kind of quaint," I told them. But I was beginning to think a little. "Look at this arena," they pointed. "Can't you call it 'Early Erector Set' like you did Minneapolis?" I looked around. "I could say I wonder where they put the dirigible while the game is going on," I admitted. They were ecstatic.

"The organist!" they yelled. "Isn't it terrible the way she plays chords when the home team scores and dirges when the visitors do?" I had to admit they had something there.

I concentrated on the game. The Spokane Comets are by all odds the dirtiest team in the league. They have one player who makes Pretty Boy Floyd look like a Scout leader. On ice he does, anyway. Con Madigan spent more time in the penalty box than he did on the rink. Their ace defense man, Bill Shvetz, hits more people over the head than a waterfront shore patrolman and Jon Arnett would like to get some of the blocks they put on the Blades' skaters. Madigan threw Jean Marc Picard so high once it looked like a lift-off at Cape Kennedy. Willie O'Ree had so many ribs separated in five minutes he won't be able to breathe deep till Easter.

"That's not a hockey team down there. That's the Capone gang!" I shouted. "These guys should play all their home games at San Quentin."

There was a strange silence. My acquaintances looked at

me suddenly with baleful eyes. Then they spoke. "What are you, a Southern California wise guy?" they snarled. "Who do you think you are, coming up here and knocking our hockey team? Why don't you put on your dark glasses and your suede shoes and go back where you belong with the rest of those Hollywood phonies."

A Day on the Beach

From my home on the beach, I can look out on a hot summer's weekend and see an endless chain of California humanity on the shore. At first glance, it looks as if Vic Tanny's has sprung a big leak. I mean, you have never seen such beautiful people. Golden tans. Bulging muscles. Seaweed for hair. Celery tonic and Metrecal popsicles for lunch. No wonder Georgie Jessel and Little Orphan Annie never get any older when they live in this outdoor Eden.

The girls all look like Brigitte Bardot. Come to think of it, some of the men do, too.

The beaches are beautiful. The climate, as usual, is in a rut. Bright sunshine. Blue water. Surfboards bobbing on the horizon. When you know that everyone out there is full of health-giving orange juice, you suddenly realize you are looking at the greatest collection of vitamin C in the western world and you begin to get ashamed of the Scotch-and-soda in your hand. "Honey," you call out, "throw this Scotch-and-soda away, will you, and bring me a vodka and orange juice?"

There's another thing that makes you feel guilty when you contemplate the mounds of glowing torsos out there.

If it weren't for the lifeguards on the beaches, some of them would never leave there. I admit they couldn't pick a lovelier spot for it. But to die full of vitamin C seems an awful cheat.

In the past ten years, the lifeguards on our beaches have rescued more than 25,000 bathers from drowning and you can't help thinking what a mess the shore would be if they hadn't. It would have more bodies than tin cans—if that's possible.

The guy who named our ocean the "Pacific" had one hell of a sense of humor. He's probably the same guy who first called a bald-headed man "Curly." Our ocean is a nasty-tempered beast of prey which will turn on you without warning. I was talking to Zuma Beach lifeguard captain Bob Burnside about it.

"People tend to think of the Pacific as one big swimming pool," he admitted. "Well, if you fill the pool with sharks, killer whale, barracuda, riptides, lateral currents, undertows, submerged wreckage and runaway surfboards, you have something like it. Throw in some hidden rocks and an octopus and it's closer yet."

I made a mental note to give the idea to Chas. Addams for a cartoon and began to press Bob for an idea of how ready our lifeguards are to combat this watery man-killer.

It's funny thing, when most people think of a lifeguard, they think of a gorgeous hunk of muscles whiling away the summer vacation sitting on a high chair on the beach with a golden tan and a whistle around his neck keeping a sharp lookout for sharks and bikinis with blondes in them.

His "rescues," they are sure, largely consist of breakneck dashes into two feet of water to wrap his arms around some helpless young thing who feigns a swoon to get him to ask for a date.

Instead, lifeguarding is an exacting career job which calls for a man to have the reflexes of an athlete, the rudiments of medicine and suicidal bravery. In 1953, lifeguard Dale Strand saved two girls from a circling shark by grabbing it by its fin and tail and holding on till they swam to safety. The shark didn't relish losing its dinner and took a hunk out of Strand's thigh to let him know it.

If you have ever tried to keep your eye on a Cub Scout troop at a picnic, multiply the harassment by two thousand and you have an idea of a lifeguard's Sunday afternoon. Personally, after a day of it, I could sit there and enjoy a drowning or two but a guard would rather lose his own life than a customer's. It's a point of pride.

It's not only saving their damn lives, it's putting ammonia on their kids' jellyfish burns, getting the volleyball for them, finding lost babies and giving first aid to big toes cut on booby-trap beer cans. A condition known as "tower fatigue" sets in for a man who has spent his day watching these clumsy landlubbers maim, burn, or drown themselves in an afternoon—sometimes all three.

It's not the daring swimmers that give the most concern. These are witless fellows known to the lifeguard service as "channel-swimmers" but they can be picked up when they get in trouble—and they do—by the bay watch boat.

It's the shoreline waders, known to the guards as "hip-booters" that have to be closely watched. For one thing, there's so many of them. For another, they are in so shallow they are ignorantly oblivious to the danger. "People have drowned in water they could stand up in," Bob Burnside told me. "And they can be in serious trouble within two or three yards of another swimmer and he won't even notice it."

The guard looks first for the telltale "ladder climb," the

frantic pawing of the swimmer in panic. A man who starts that is about to become a statistic.

Next in order of peril are the "drugstore frogmen," the happy-go-lucky refugees from a swimming pool who pick up skindiving equipment at bargain drug counters. Over 99 percent of the drownings off the coast of California are due to inexpert use of Scuba apparatus. The equipment is found in perfect working condition, but the swimmer is drowned, the five-fathom equivalent of a successful surgery the patient doesn't stick around to applaud. "Putting these drugstore frogmen loose on the bottom is like letting a monkey drive a car on the freeway," notes Burnside.

Parents who put kids on inner tubes make guards bitter, too. "They won't trust them on the wheels of their car but they'll trust them under their kids on the ocean."

Lifeguards stay in shape with regular inter-station competitions—like the recent "Taplin Award" races at Hermosa Beach, a salt-water decathlon in which teams from stations up and down the Coast compete in hairbreadth relay swims, surfboard matches and four-oared dory dashes where big, 300-pound whaleboats, about as manageable in high surf as a mustang with a burr under his tail, struggle to pin the riders under their raging hulks of lumber. To survive is honor enough. To win, as Zuma did, is a signal achievement.

It's a strange thing, the guards say, but some swimmers die without emotion, as if they're ashamed of themselves for being so gauche. All I can say is, don't be afraid to yell "Help!" These guys are ready.

Now the sun is high and hot over the horse latitudes, the winter rains have left, the jellyfish have come back, and it's time again for that most popular of all sports—a day at the seashore.

The sharks again will be abroad on the shoreline eagerly awaiting the schools of human center cuts in rubber suits which Nature, in its infinite mystery, sees fit to provide just as the sardine seem to disappear.

A number of the rest of you will also join the human tides that sweep to the sea this time of the year, not to feed the sharks, but to clutter the sand in search of peeled noses, parbroiled backs, slashed big toes and sand in the sandwiches.

The sharks are elated. But we established beachcombers of the sunlit littoral view the annual migration with all the enthusiasm usually reserved for gas on the stomach—or a dog about to catch a fresh set of fleas. Helpless but resigned.

For those of you who are visiting our lovely shores for the first time, who have come to us from the well-mannered communities of St. Louis, Kansas City, Cincinnati, or Tulsa, we have prepared a handy tourist guide, a behavioral signpost the better to aid you in enjoying your stay on the sunny strand. The first thing to remember is to forget everything you have ever been taught about being a thoughtful guest.

When you get to the sea, you must get as close to becoming a human shark—in or out of the water—as possible. Bad manners are as essential as sun-tan lotion for a truly happy day at the beach. Here are the handy hints to follow:

1—Be sure to take your inner tubes. They collapse at the touch of a rock and sink like one and take you with them. This prevents the lifeguards from getting flabby.

2—Take your trash along. If you can't dump it on the

beach, find the nearest residential front lawn. The people who live there will pick it up. They have to. If they don't, the county will fine them for littering the landscape.

3—When you get home, if you find someone has dropped even a gum wrapper on *your* lawn, call the cops.

4—If you're a teenager, be sure to leave your breeding at home. Use language your father would lock you in the woodshed for and, above all, show no respect for womanhood. If some parent complains, pick four of the biggest guys with you and ask him if he wants to make something out of it.

5—If you bring the old folks along, pick a seat along side a crowd of these teenagers. That way, you won't have to read *Tropic of Cancer*, after all.

6—Bring the dogs. They liven things up enormously. They throw sand, help themselves to other people's lunch, bark and have a helluva time. Also, they fight with each other. Dogs turn a day at the seashore into a rumble on the docks. If things go well, someone will probably get bitten which helps the day pass quickly. And don't worry about it: statistics show most dogs don't have rabies.

7—If you bring a surfboard, be sure to aim it at the nearest knot of small children. Their scalps cut easier and they can't get out of the way as fast.

8—If you have any leftovers, dispose of it on the highway. There's a fine for this, but the cops will be too busy trying to unsnarl the traffic you have caused. Besides, it's better to drop it out the window than take it home and clog your disposal when the coast highway will serve as well.

9—If you bring small children, and you will, don't arrange a common meeting place if you get lost. That way, you will deprive the lifeguards of hours of enjoyable searching up and down the beach with a crying baby.

10—If the guards yell, "Everybody out of the water!" don't pay any attention to them. Those guys are always crying "Wolf!" or at least "Shark!" The first fin they see, they panic. Stand up for your rights. After all, you're a taxpayer. Keep telling yourself no one can push you around just because he's got a little tin whistle. Besides, it's well known sharks are cowards and taxpayers aren't. That's why sharks eat taxpayers.

11—Horseplay is always a good idea. You not only cover the potato salad with sand but three chances out of three someone will get hurt. Don't let that stop you. The lifeguards are expert at applying tourniquets.

12—If you bring a girl, neck up a storm—particularly if there're little kids watching. Never mind if you look like a poster from an Italian movie. It's a free country, isn't it?

13—If you do all these things, do one other—No. 13: Tie a rock around your neck and jump in. For me. And Bon Voyage!

Husing Signs Off

Cy Rice, the author, was on the phone. He sounded heartbroken. "Ted's dead," he said. "Ted Husing. Did you know him?"

Did I know him? It was like asking a man if he remembered his childhood. I had met Ted, sure; a perfunctory, pointless introduction to a blind, crippled man who had no way of knowing the special evocative meaning the very sound of his voice had.

Husing was, to put it simply, the greatest. He was to

broadcasting what Grange was to football, Ruth to baseball, Dempsey to boxing, Lardner to writing. He was the
voice that brought the special surge of glamour to the
quackery of sportscasting.

"Good afternoon, everyone, everywhere," Husing would
crackle into a microphone and 40,000,000 people would settle back for four hours of soothing excitement. It was a
funny thing, but you remembered a game Husing broadcast
better than a game you saw in person. He made a Notre
Dame-Ohio State game the most famous football match of
a generation once by the quality of his description.

I heard the famous Harvard-Yale broadcast where Ted
described, not Harvard's playing as legend has it, but Barry
Wood's playing as "putrid." The Harvard quarterback had
destroyed Army, 14–13, only a week or so before and Ted, in
the broadcasters' booth, was frustrated for him. Yale, of
course, had set their defenses for this lone capable football
player in the Harvard backfield. But Ted and 40,000 fans
didn't appreciate this. His unfortunate choice of adjective
which was typically graphic brought the wrath of fair Harvard on him. Among those unimpressed was the columnist,
Heywood Broun. "Just another example of the menace Harvard poses to human liberty," he sniffed. And Harvard sub-
sided abruptly.

Ted Husing went through life with a quip on his lips,
a Racing Form in his pocket and he leaked money. He was
an enthusiastic and paid-up member of what one writer
called "the lonely crowd" of Manhattan of the Thirties. Ted
thought he had more friends than he could count. No one
does. His life was a tragedy only because it lasted seven
years too long.

It was in 1956 that Ted awakened in a hospital in New
York. It was an upset for him to be anywhere but at "21"

that late in the day. His sensations were recorded in his remarkable biography, *My Eyes Are in My Heart*. "Who am
I?" was his first question. He couldn't see, but he was sure
it was just temporary. It wasn't. It was forever. "I hope
you're not too beautiful," he joked with his nurse, "because when they take these bandages off, I might never
want to leave." There was a silence. "Mr. Husing," the
nurse told him awkwardly. "There are no bandages on your
eyes."

There were bandages on Ted Husing's eyes most of his
life, but he never found it out until he couldn't see. When
he finally lived out his life entombed in the wreckage of his
own body he came, too late, to understand.

He was born the son of a German saloonkeeper. On his
mother's side, he was Jewish, but Ted didn't care for the
sensation. Only later did he come to appreciate the priceless
heritage of three thousand years of culture and refinement
that helped make little Edward Britt Husing become Ted
Husing. In his salad years Ted Husing elected to go with
the barbarians.

Ralph Edwards once said "Marconi invented radio but
Ted Husing knew what to do with it." His was a love affair with the medium that left no room for rivals. He lost a
lovely wife and family in his mad pursuit of the bubble,
fame, but it wasn't the hours on microphone Husing was
later to begrudge, it was the hours in the Stork Club. "It
wasn't for a long time that I became mature enough to understand that New Year's Eve is much more fun if you
don't try to throw a party every night," he wrote. That a
radio broadcaster had to be seen as well as heard was his
wrong notion.

He got his own tailor as soon as he got his own microphone. "Make me look like a celebrity," he commanded. His

lack of formal education gave him a thirst for a vocabulary a Harvard professor might envy. He puddled the language of sport. He not only introduced the football fans to a "secondary" defense, he even invented a "tertiary," a position formerly known as safety man. A ball-carrier was never merely tackled. He was hit by "a whole host" of tacklers. Nobody ever heard of a "half-host" but with Husing, it didn't matter. He was Caruso, Verdi, and Toscanini all wrapped in one. So far as his fans were concerned, he invented the sport.

He played other roles in the formation of radio networks. There were mishaps. Queen Marie of Rumania came to this country with her hand out—not for friendship, for money. NBC crossed it with gold for her to appear on behalf of Royal typewriters, of all things. At the last minute, the Queen abdicated the broadcast, overthrown by an outraged Long Island society matron who didn't need the money herself. Husing was unaware. "Ladies and gentlemen, I give you—the Queen of Rumania," he shouted coast-to-coast. And out walked David Sarnoff.

He called a Kentucky Derby right the year Lawrin won it only because he had made a winter book bet (of $4,300) on the winner and like every other punter he was only watching his own horse. NBC incorrectly identified Blue Larkspur as the winner.

We all begin to die the moment we are born. But in Ted's case he could watch it. In horrible fascination. He noticed it, of all places, in his shoes. He began to drag his right foot. His right shoe wore out months before his other one.

The rest of Ted Husing wore out, too. There came a day when he became a disc jockey—and an entire industry should have held its head in shame. He became cranky, critical. Friends walked away from him. At a time he needed them most.

There came a day when he was walking down a Manhattan street and it disappeared on him. "An earthquake," thought Ted Husing. Seconds later, he knew it wasn't. "The chaos was inside Ted Husing," he wrote sadly.

The chaos always had been. But it was a wonderful chaotic magic that gave a focus and meaning to the mindless static, squawks and bleeps that was early-day radio. Ted said goodbye to everyone, everywhere. He died in a rest home in Pasadena. But he can never die in the hearts of those who heard him in his great days when he was in love with America and it with him—when the leaves were turning and frost was in the air and he was describing what he christened "the annual autumnal madness of football."

"Some day, somewhere, some man might get as good as Ted Husing was," Red Smith once wrote. "But I doubt it." Ted himself said: "I no longer see . . . but I can feel. Today, I don't need eyes in my head. My eyes are in my heart." So, today, are ours. Only, our eyes are wet.

Edge of Sadness

I remember the first time I heard a great concert pianist and I realized with a pang that my whole life had been wasted. No one had ever told me—or convinced me, anyway—that such beauty could be produced by the hand of man. More than anything in the world, I wanted to be that man.

I saw Barrymore when he was still Barrymore, Spencer

Tracy immersing himself in a role until by the middle of the picture, he wasn't Tracy any more but the man he was playing—and I wanted to be a great actor.

The first time I saw *Carmen* was on a ratty, outdoor stage in a New England amusement park with a company of screech owls and a derisive audience. But it didn't matter. It was still *Carmen*. I wished I had written it.

I heard Caruso and, even on an old acoustical record, the thrill was there. I wanted to be able to break chandeliers with a single note. I saw Toulouse-Lautrec's posters and I envied him. It didn't matter that he was a legless, alcoholic runt. God had more than made it up to him.

I wanted to hit a tennis ball like Jack Kramer. I longed to be Ben Hogan. I saw Dempsey and even Liston and thought what a marvelous thing to be able to walk down the street and know that no human being would harm you. I saw Duke Snider and Ted Williams and I wished I were left-handed. I saw DiMaggio and I was glad I wasn't.

But nobody ever made me want to be a basketball player until I saw Elgin Baylor. The poetry, drama, and meaning of the game eluded me until he made it all clear.

Bob Cousy I admired as I might admire a magician—or a cut purse. He had the daring, the color. But he stole the ball, and points, like a marmoset snatching the bait without disturbing the trap.

Elgin Baylor came on court like a lion, not a marmoset. The field scattered before him like a crap game when the law appears. Elgin scorned cunning, emotionalism, stealth. He took points as if they belonged to him.

Elgin was a hero you could sink your teeth into. "Go in on him, I dare ya," his friends would taunt all the registered monsters of the league. Elgin was as unstoppable as a woman's tears.

He came only 6 ft. 5 and he was a forward. So he was never the bully. There will never be another 6-foot 5-incher in the front court in this league because there will never be another Baylor. What he did was right out in the open and thrilling.

Bill Russell is a great defensive player, but what he does under the basket is as hard to see as Texas chiggers—as Bill intends. There are times when he not only doesn't want the crowd to see, he doesn't even want the officials to see. Wilt Chamberlain scored in the upper reaches, but Wilt was in the upper reaches himself. Any taller and you could hold the Winter Olympics on his summit.

But a terrible thing has happened. Hardly anyone wants to be Elgin Baylor any more. A few little pieces of calcium above the left knee and suddenly the concert pianist is off-key and hitting clunkers. He sounds as if he's playing with boxing gloves. Caruso is hitting sharp and flat notes. The chandelier doesn't even tremble. *Carmen* is just a toothless old bag. Dempsey can't win a fight with his wife. Snider can't get around on a fast ball.

The lion has a thorn in his paw.

It's heartbreaking to see the jackals come out of the woodwork of the forest, teeth bared, laughing. Guys who used to fake a head cold on the nights they needed to stop Baylor now volunteer. They set a Farmer on him here at St. Louis, Mike Farmer. But any farmer might do. They might have tried a plumber or a ribbon clerk. Because Elg is not Elg. He's still one of the top ten scorers of the league. For anyone else, it would be cause for throwing a dinner. For Elg, they call in the Mayo Clinic.

For years, he has never been lower than second. Only Wilt outscored him. From a 38-point average two years ago, he's dipped below 25. He used to drive under the basket with such contemptuous ease that only a silver bullet would stop him. On nights when the defense would be bunched like a goal-line stand, Elg would simply pop in from outside. He could throw the ball the length of the court on a line. The Lakers called him "Edge" because he was the cutting half of their sword.

But the edge has been dulled and the Lakers couldn't cut butter. When Elg can't get inside under the basket these nights, his jump shot looks like a man trying to get out of quicksand with overshoes on.

It's like watching Tilden lob the ball up to the net or a bird bravely flying with a broken wing. It's like Joe Louis throwing the famous left and stepping back. But the other guy doesn't fall, he laughs.

The chagrin is league-wide. Because people loved to see Baylor hit a basket the way they loved to see Musial hit a baseball.

It's sad to speak of Elg in the past tense. When it happens gradually, you get used to it. The average athlete sets like the sun. Baylor dropped like a rock. It is the story of this Laker trip east. For Elg, this place should be called "St. Louis, Misery." He is like a bowed-tendon horse hitched to a wagon of bricks and asked to pull it uphill in the snow. The doctors are in disagreement as to the efficacy of an operation. But they are all in agreement on one thing, that the odds are not good that Baylor will ever be Baylor again. He may only be a reasonable facsimile.

It's not enough. If I want Rembrandt, I don't want him on an insurance calendar. I don't want Caruso forced to sing "Melancholy Baby," Paderewski needing a metronome. If the sawbones can't put Baylor back together the way I want to remember him, I don't want him to be a basketball player any more. I want the unreasonable facsimile, the real thing. The lion, not the leopard. The "Edge," not the handle.

The Artist's Last Tour

They brought the Mona Lisa to this country and people knocked down doors to get to look at it for five seconds. Sarah Bernhardt made more "final" appearances than your wife's brother. Caruso had to die on it before they let him off stage. They would flock to see Paderewski even if he were soloing on a player piano.

Only in sports do we let our works of art and working artists fade out like old light bulbs while the claque rushes off in hot pursuit of the incandescence of a new one. Babe Ruth ended his career in the inglorious uniform of the Boston Braves, rapping an occasional home run in the National League hinterland before a select audience of umpires, ushers, and a few other people who had nothing better to do that afternoon.

Joe Louis hit the tank towns as a wrestling referee. Some once-great pitchers have been found in flea-bag hotel rooms, their only companions a bottle of rotgut. Jim Thorpe was digging a ditch.

This, then, is to warn you that if you want to get a last look at the artist in art it behooves you to get out to the Sports Arena this weekend. Robert Joseph Cousy, the best 6 ft. 1 in. artist in a basketball suit who ever lived, will be giving his final seasonal recital, a fugue for two hands, two legs and one basket. Like Bernhardt, he may be back—but only in the playoffs, a promise as chimerical as a Hollywood marriage in which several things have to break just right in a 16-dog-and-cat fight.

Perhaps it is presumptuous to compare a mere athlete, a basketball player at that, to a work of art. Perhaps Bob Cousy is more Boston Pops and Arthur Fiedler than Arturo Toscanini, more comic strip than a candidate for the Louvre, a rhyme, not a poem. But anyone who has ever seen him with a basketball in his hand when the action was fluid, the juices flowing and the stakes high, would have to doubt it. Art is something that moves you or exhilarates or excites or disturbs, that lifts you out of yourself. If you are in a position to appreciate artistry in sport at all, if you are not athletically tone-deaf or color-blind, Bob Cousy does all of these things.

The cold type of the catalogue clearly points to artistry not academic. The florid records, like most points scored, most field goals attempted, most rebounds made, belong to the registered Leaning Towers of the league. The pastel tones, like "Most assists per game" belong to Bob Cousy— "28, Boston vs. Minneapolis 2/27/59." Most assists per half-game and per quarter-game also belong to Cousy. Someone has to get the ball for the dunkers, hang it up there by the basket where they can reach over and slap it in. Someone has to dribble the ball around the court when the hour is late and the lead is short and the floor is full of enemy players snapping at the ball like human barracuda.

Someone has to play to win a game rather than set a record. This is Bob Cousy.

Cousy was one of the first to dribble behind the back without losing possession of the ball. He was not the first but the best at leading a fast break down the floor like the first con in a prison bust-out. He is a flying blur with a basketball in his hand and a look on his face as if the game is lowermost in his mind and what he's really trying to concentrate on is what his wife told him to bring home for dinner. Suddenly there's a whoosh! and a 78 ft. pass is orbiting over the basket, an easy 2-point tap-in for Tom Heinsohn, Satch Sanders, one of the Jones boys, one of the Celts.

A year from today, Bob Cousy will be in a sweat suit in a musty gym in Boston teaching some college boys the fine arts of a fine game. It's a game which has been good to him but the opposite is true, also, and it is a game which has been good to a lot of people who didn't reciprocate.

The Celts didn't even want Bob Cousy when he first came out of Holy Cross, a baker's dozen years ago. He was too short and too slow, they said.

It was the narrowest escape any sport ever had. Picture leaving Red Grange on an ice truck or Babe Ruth in an orphan asylum and you have the idea. If there had been no Cousy then, there might be no basketball today. He not only set a record for assists on the floor, he did it off, too. His most important records were set in banquets attended, kids helped, time given. He not only assisted games of basketball, he assisted the institution of basketball.

I have a personal measure of the class of Bob Cousy. In my time, I have gotten exactly three letters of appreciation from athletes I have written about. The first of these was from Bob Cousy. On or off the court his works are art.

He can't play long anymore. But for nineteen minutes, you'll think there's two of him out there. So will the guy guarding him. It'll be nineteen minutes of Rembrandt basketball on its last triumphal tour. You'll want to brag some day you saw it.

OFF-BROADWAY SPORTS

The "Little Sports"

This is a section some editors choose to call the "Little Sports." English translation: sports people would rather play than watch.

A fat man with a pool cue. A sandy game of volleyball on the beach. A day with the lifeguards. A man's uncle with a pool chalk and a deck of cards.

One is not sure whether they're "sports" or just a way to get out of doing the dishes.

To a writer, they're a special challenge. Up further in this tome, you may have read (with tears in your eyes) my apologia for the sportswriter. How he serves humanity and preserves the expense account.

But, making a character out of Frank Howard (where, as the poet says, Nature anticipated me) and making readability out of a thing which must be done rather than watched are two vastly different things.

The eminently readable Paul Gallico, in his valedictory to the press box, "Farewell to Sport," once noted with some surprise that lacrosse "wasn't a bad game to watch." He used to skip Army football to go over and take it in. But he presumably found explaining it to his readership, or making it universally entertaining, just too much of a task.

So it is with the "little sports." They take reserves of writing strength and dramatization that are just too much for the man who must grind out one of these works a day. It is so much easier to start a column "Don Drysdale yesterday . . ." and *know* you have your readership's enthralled attention.

And yet "little sports" include the stupendous adventure of climbing Everest. They include the lore of the sea, the challenge of sail and wind against storm and sharks, the fantastic saga of the mightiest of earth's creatures, the whales, returning to their ancestral spawning grounds by some alchemy of nature that defies terrestrial comprehension.

A boy and a surfboard is as much the stuff of drama as a man and a bat. It takes a bit of doing, is all. The reader must be beguiled into the tent in the first couple of paragraphs or lost for twenty-four hours. "I never read you when you write about golf," a man tells you smugly. You resist the temptation to tell him you'll never eat carrots again if he's a green grocer, or to tell him you think insurance is a lot of humbug if he's an underwriter.

The "little sports" give me my greatest pleasure as a writer. I think a man who wants to stay with football and baseball is a man who wants to stay with meat and potatoes. Reading—even sports page reading—should be exploring.

Sports, of course, isn't theology. The chances are, skywriting will last as long and loom as large in literature. But I submit, the "little sports" are not the weeds in the garden of athletics. They are the blossoms.

Bob Cousy, that superb practitioner of a "little sport," that became a big one, i. e., professional basketball, once noted wistfully that *his* sport had a hard row to hoe because it was in competition with baseball which had a sixty-year-head-start on the sports page and thus what Cooz wisely called "a fifty-year bin of anecdotal lore" to draw on to bury basketball under a ton of adjectives and funny stories.

But the man who plays volleyball—or lacrosse—or who sails or golfs—*loves* his sport with a passion that the hired athlete can never muster for *his* sport. That's because the pro athlete's sport is also his work. The carpenter does not rhapsodize about hanging a door. The plumber does not compose a sonnet to a Roto-Rooter. The second-baseman who gets paid for plumbing second base and doing woodwork at home plate is no less. "There's nothing to smile about when you put on this uniform," Jim Gilliam once growled at a photographer who aimed at him before a night game and said "Now, smile a little, please."

It was Lincoln or Mark Twain, I forget who, who said "God must have loved the poor people, he made so many of them." So it is with "little sports." There are horseshoe pitchers who take their sport entirely seriously, exchange literature, mount an annual "world" championship, and, in general, have a helluva time. There is a fly-casting champion and every responsible fly-caster knows who he is. There is a man (and a woman) who has caught the biggest marlin ever caught. And every fisherman worthy of the name knows who he and she is.

The question is, to find what motivates "little" sportsman. I think I know, or can divine, the feelings of the home-run hero who is at bat with the count 3-and-2 and the crowd screaming and the World Series at stake. It has to be panic. He lives with panic, and he just might hit the home run despite the small knot of fear in his stomach. He has learned to swing a bat by reflex.

But how do I know what exhilaration a dragster feels as he tools a home-made roadster through a slot at 100-miles-plus per hour from a standing start in a quarter-mile? How can I *really* know the euphoria of topping off a hitherto-un-climbable mountain? My head is hanging over the rail on yacht rides, not scanning the stars for navigational clues.

But I sense the joy. And I envy. It would never occur to me to envy either the pitcher or the batter in a two-outs situation in the World Series. Nor do I wish to be the full-back who has to carry the ball through the Green Bay Packers on the one-yard line with 20 seconds to play.

But when I see groups of happy people cheerfully gather, at their own expense, for an evening of Karate, or volleyball, or horseshoe-pitching, or fly-casting, or surf-casting, or bil-liards—I do envy.

I want to tell people about them and about the thing that makes them happy. It, too, isn't easy. The guy who says "I never read you when you write about golf" is liable to stop looking altogether if you start writing about la-crosse. I personally am addicted to whale-watching. By geography. They go right past my front door.

I also like to talk to Norman Dhyhrenfurth about what it's like on the roof of the world—Everest. I think a man who dons a face-mask and dives down where only dead men have gone before him has a wildly exciting story to tell.

I like sports. And they include "little sports."

Coyote Calling

Are you having trouble with your neighborhood coyotes? Do they keep sitting around and staring when you have company?

Bobcats tearing up the patio furniture? Foxes fighting

under the window when you're trying to watch the Late Show? And how about mountain lions? Getting in the petunia bulbs again?

Guard against all this by getting in touch immediately via the Yellow Pages with your friendly courteous varmint caller. Rid your washday worries of animal acts. At absolutely no cost to you he will call up every four-footed chicken killer in your block and cart them out feet first.

This modern Pied Piper is never happier than when he is giving a concert on a tiny whistle for an audience of the blood-thirstiest crew of predators he can draw around him. When they are sufficiently mesmerized, he calmly kills them.

It's not the music that soothes the savage breasts. It's the promise of instant dinner on the hoof. The varmint caller's wood-wind looses on the air a cry of distress that sounds on the night air like a cross between the cry of a dog with its tail caught in the door and the whimper of a woman who sees another woman at a party wearing the same dress. The varmints come not to help but to eat.

Douglas Kittredge, age thirty-six, one of the foremost callers in the country and an archer of note, once took time out to demonstrate for me the finer points of this arcane art.

Doug has socialized in his time with more wild animals than Tarzan. He takes up his stand after nightfall in any wooded area where the varmints hang out, douses himself with garlic oil so the animals will be deceived into thinking there's no human scent or the distressed prey has been into the lasagna again.

Doug also wears a beard which helps to conceal the inner man, too, and sometimes the varmint—including the coyote, one of the smartest old dogs in the world—comes all the way face-to-face with Doug before it dawns on them that no rabbit wears eyeglasses. By then, it's too late. Sometimes the animal reacts violently to this cheap deceit and varmint callers have been known to get a bite on the nose from a furious fox. Even in the best of conditions, it is unwise to poke one's nose out of the blind lest it meet a cold one coming in.

Occasionally, a "peccary" or "javelina," or wild hog, is moved to investigate the cry for help and the caller has to move fast or find himself instead of the perambulating ham sandwich the main course. A caller dredged up a mountain lion one night and found himself standing before it foolishly with nothing but a .22 and a flashlight, neither of which is very handy in a fight with a lion.

Kittredge stumbled on this unique form of a baited hunt when the manufacturer of the magic whistles, a dude from Texas, wandered into Kittredge's archery store in Glendale some years ago. He proposed that they go out and get up a party of furry friends. He was dressed all in white from boots to ten-gallon hat and looked so much like something that had fallen off a Christmas tree that Kittredge protested he would scare more animals out of the woods than a forest fire.

Tex streaked up the hills with his blinding hunting clothes intact, put his whistle to his lips and soon had enough coyotes around him for two rubbers of bridge and enough foxes to make a coat.

Kittredge hunts in more conventional raiment but the varmints don't mind. All they have to be is hungry and apparently they eat more often than truck drivers because Doug has never had a failure. In fact, he leaves the impression he could summon a convention of wolves to the top floor of the Biltmore if they could find the elevator.

The sound he puts down would never do for The Twist. "It's a kind of universal distress cry. The animal can't tell what it is but it sounds good to eat."

Coyotes come on the double. You can hear their feet pounding on the hard ground for miles. Fox and bobcats are more subtle and sometimes the caller is as surprised to see them as they are to see him.

A coyote must be killed instantly. If he gets away he has been known to scoot at 45 m.p.h., a clocking that would get him in the winner's circle at Santa Anita with no trouble. And once fooled, he never comes to that window again. "You have to wait for his pups," Kittredge admits.

Kittredge, who is the most ardent believer in the bow-and-arrow since Sitting Bull, prefers to dispatch his daytime quarry with it but admits that at night it's more chancy since the trajectory of the arrow cannot be accurately gauged—which may be why Indians rarely fought at night.

Doug blew a few quavering notes in a Wilshire Boulevard restaurant at lunch for me but try as I could to pierce the gloom I couldn't see any pair of glowing eyes. Shook up the bartender, though, who kept shining his flashlight down on the bottom of the bar-stools to see if one of his customers had retired for the night. Several others switched to soft drinks after looking queerly at their neighbors.

We tried it in the parking lot—a hoarse bleat, then a diminishing whine. But all that came was a cop. At home, I tried it in an empty lot—and twenty-six dogs showed up.

There are some 25,000 active varmint callers in our midst, according to Kittredge. The technique is not new, to be sure. The sound and promise of fresh free food has brought in-laws on the double throughout history. Trouble is, unlike other varmints, they're never in season and you can't just hang them on your trophy wall with a sign saying, "Two tusked, white-fanged, long-billed species of North American unemployed brother-in-law—called and mounted with fake scent of chicken frying on April 1, 1962, at the dinner hour."

C'Est la Vie

There are only a few games I know where the lines of communication between the fan and the athlete are garbled.

I mean, in boxing, when the fellow says, "Get the other eye, Maxie!" Maxie knows precisely what he means. Similarly, in baseball, when someone yells, "Stick it in his ear, Don!" the batter knows immediately what to expect. "Throw the ball, ya sap!" brings a rush of color to the cheeks of quarterback Zeke Bratkowski and, "Well struck, old boy!" indicates a wicket no longer sticky.

But the ancient and honorable sport of ice hockey, it always seemed to me, was one whose practitioners were not getting the full, rich benefit of directives from the stands in the U.S. because they were in an alien tongue.

This is because the players—and the inventors of the sport—were French-Canadians, and I remembered from my childhood that French-Canadians speak a kind of fractured French that only another French-Canadian can completely comprehend.

Accordingly, I brought my friend Emile Jenest to the Blades game with me the other night. Emile is an actor with Walt Disney but most of all he is a French-Canadian and a hockey fan—which is redundant because there is no such animal as a French-Canadian who isn't. French-Canada is a place where you can call Brigitte Bardot ugly and General de Gaulle forty kinds of a bum and nobody will look up. But, just suggest Maurice "The Rocket" Richard or Benny "Boom-Boom" Geoffrion are not the greatest hockey players who ever lived and you better learn to fight with your feet.

I wanted mostly to study Emile's cheer-leader technique. I had envisioned him peppering the Sports Arena air with Gallicisms like *"Sacre Bleu!"* or *"A Bas Les Seals!"* I expected to spend the evening composing mental subtitles but I was also ready with a few supplementary exhortations of my own from my high school French like, *"Donnez-lui un coup avec le puck, Marcel!"* or, *"Mettez le puck dans le net, s'il vous plait"* even though they seem to lose something in the translation to the French.

I took out my French-English dictionary as I slid alongside Emile in our mezzanine seats and waited expectantly for the first explosion of rink-side French.

"Hergesheimer, you're a bum!" was Emile's first roar before the face-off had cleared. The San Francisco Seals scored in a minute and forty seconds. Emile buried his head in his hands and groaned. "My lord!" he moaned. "They can't even skate!" *"Mon Dieu,"* I found myself correcting him. Emile looked up. "What's that?" he asked. *"Mon Dieu,"* I said. "You should say 'Mon Dieu,' shouldn't you?" He gave me a funny look.

The action caught his eye again. "Look at that Goyer!" he roared. "He's not back-checking. Goyer, get back there, you bum!" *"Cochon,"* I corrected him. "You should say 'cochon.'" He gave me another funny look. I riffled through the dictionary looking for "Common Slang Expressions Used in Everyday French."

Another goal splattered in. "Hergesheimer, where the hell were you?" screamed Emile. "*Ou ettez vous, Monsieur Hergesheimer?*" I found myself thinking.

"In Montreal, they play this game in the Forum. Right across from a hospital," Emile confided. "It's a lucky thing, too. I saw a man get a skate right across his hand and sever it one night." "*Pauvre garçon!*" I murmured. "What?" asked Emile suspiciously. "Oh," I said hastily, "poor fellow. Did he lose his hand?"

"No," said Emile. "But he had to be careful shaking hands for a few days." I nodded my head. I could understand and could see it right now: someone might come up to him and say, "Give me your hand" and if he weren't careful he might do just that.

The action swirled on the ice below. "Shoot, dammit!" bellowed Emile. He pointed out a player. "That," he said, "is Chevrefils—Real Chevrefils, an absolutely first-class player." "That name means 'son-of-a-goat,' doesn't it?" I murmured. Emile looked thoughtful. "Yes," he acknowledged, "I suppose it does. I never thought of it."

Behind us, someone was casting even more doubt on Chevrefils' ancestry. But Emile was on his feet again. "Get back and check, you dummy!" he shrieked. He sat down in a rage. "That Hergesheimer! He couldn't put a puck in an open sea!" he gritted. "Play 'The Skater's Waltz' for those bums," he instructed the organist in a howl. "What is this, a minuet?"

He turned to me and brightened. "It's a great game, isn't it?" he enthused. I sighed and put away my dictionary. "Yeah, Emile, it's a gas," I told him. Emile leaned forward. "A what?" he asked. "A 'gas,'" I told him. "It's an old French expression. You wouldn't understand."

Off and Running

There are over 6,000,000 people who attend horse races annually in the state of California and they are like no other breed, animal, vegetable or mineral, anywhere on earth.

They are the largest congress of philanthropists in the western world. Thanks to the cut the state takes of their wagers, they donate to charity, build schools, finance county fairs, underwrite employment for boys handicapped by size, and restore wildlife. The next time you see an elk grazing on a state preserve, just remember that behind every elk stands a guy with frayed cuffs and holes in his shoes smoking a cigar stub he just rescued from an ash-can by the $2 window.

A racetrack crowd comprises the greatest floating fund of misinformation this side of the pages of *Pravda*, the last virgin stand of optimism in our century.

They get back eighty-five cents on the dollar but they don't complain. Anywhere else this happened, they'd send for the Better Business Bureau.

They look unhappy but they're not. They're where they want to be, doing what they want to do—lose. A psychologist has said that the underlying compulsive wish of any gambler was to lose and the racetrackers are only too glad the track is there to oblige them.

When they get mad, it's not the money. They lose $2,

they'll spend $5 buying you a drink explaining why it shouldn't have happened. They are not matching money. They are matching wits—with horses, who have the lowest form of intelligence of any of God's creatures. With the possible exception of horse-players.

They have a lingo all of their own. It sounds plausible but it is a trap. It is designed to appeal to the larceny in you. So I deem it no more than my duty to arm you with a few handy mental retorts you should keep firmly in focus the next time one of the fraternity approaches you in the paddock.

On the left is what he will say. On the right is what you must think—or find yourself joining this forlorn but happy crew.

"I've got the horse right here." Oh, no, he hasn't.

"I don't see how he can lose." You will in a minute.

"He should tow-rope this field." A good idea because he sure can't run with them.

"He belongs in with this bunch." He belongs in with a milk truck.

"The rider change should make the difference." Where this pig will be running, snatching a few saddle cloths will only make the difference between last and next-to-last, neither of which they pay off on.

"He's had some good works." Nobody has bothered to pull a watch on him this meeting. You could clock him with a calendar. The only reason he got stall space is because the owner knows the governor and the track wants more racing dates.

"He gets weight off a good effort." If the racing secretary thought that was a good effort, he'd load him down with a hot stove, because he passes out lead like Eliot Ness. This dog got weight off because the track is afraid he'd drop dead on the post parade under a full-sized jock.

"He figures in here with these if you go back to some of his good races." If he could go back to some of his good races, he wouldn't be in here with these. He wouldn't figure in a field of lame elephants.

"I know a bookie said to chunk it in on this one." I know the bookie, too. He wants to retire to Honolulu and if he can get a few tips like this one going, he'll have it made. This beetle should be pulling a starting gate, not leaving one.

"This is an information horse." And the information is he couldn't beat his lead pony in a match race with a pull in the weights.

"He'll be a running horse today." If so, it'll be the first time this meeting. The last time the stable was trying with him, he was running away from a forest fire at the ranch.

"I didn't care for the ride the boy gave him." Neither did the film patrol. One more like that and this jock will be lucky to get a mount on a merry-go-round. But this horse runs just as slow under a whip as under a pull.

"He likes this track." He ought to. The way he runs any other track in the country would take his number down. He's knocked more horses into the fence than a rocky homestretch and cut in front of more traffic than a drunk on the freeway. He's not a runner, he's a wrestler.

"Well, we'll get 'em tomorrow." Not if the kids have hidden their piggy banks.

Boys with Green Hair

Far at sea, the earth grunts and a giant bubble of water surges to the surface.

Its emergence is of mild interest in the offices of oceanographers, meteorologists or seismologists who go on with their coffee break. But it sets off wild excitement with another, larger segment of the population. The surfers are electrified.

The great swell is tracked from shore as breathlessly as a man in orbit. The exact time of its arrival, the moment it will begin crashing in huge waves on the coast line of California, is computed with care and the word is passed along as quickly and mysteriously as the communication that tells a rat a ship is going to sink.

On the day of arrival, the Pacific Coast Highway is suddenly awash with jalopies, doodle-bugs, station wagons and convertibles speeding to the sea with stacks of boards sticking out of them like quills from a porcupine. The whacky, wonderful cult of the surfboard is on its way to the sea.

As they pull up to the Malibu Pier with a squeal of brakes and begin to pile out like clowns out of a circus car, they seem at first glance to look all alike—and not earth people at all. To begin with, their hair is green. Their bodies are muscled and hard. Their eyes have an unholy light of anticipation as they dash to the water clutching 9-foot lengths of tapered fiberglass and styro-foam that look like frozen sharks even to the fin-like keel. They slap these in the sea and then kneel on them as if in prayer.

Then, they swiftly paddle out with their arms to meet the waves . . . .

The world of the surfboarders is a world apart. Their sport is less a sport than an art form. Its appeal seems to lie in man's ancient passion to be able to walk on water. In high water, it is a ballet-like contest between man and sea that addicts say is like no other feeling in the world. "Snow-skiing approaches it," a surfer once told me with a faraway look in his eyes, "except the mountain doesn't disappear on you on the way down. That makes the difference."

The trick is to run diagonally before the curl of a wave, and a condition where a marine shelf of land juts out in the lee side of a promontory is ideal. It's dangerous and part of the charm is the exhilaration of doing something which might kill you. The higher the wave, the greater the ecstasy.

The payoff is a smooth but breakneck ride down a wall of water—or a sickening but sublime "wipe-out" when board and man meet the water wrong and it splatters them both in its boiling white center. The board squirts skyward like a fish climbing a hatchery ladder and its keel, or "skeg," is a cleaver gleaming in the sun waiting to cut through flesh or bone. The high surf brings, in addition to exhilaration, broken noses, cracked knees, cut eyes, scalp wounds.

The summit of surfing is the Big Surf at Makaha on Oahu where the cultists make an annual pilgrimage, some to compete in the World Series of surfing, others to sit on the beach in palm frond hats with ukuleles and cameras to get in on the fun and guffaw at the wipe-outs. At Makaha, these are as awesome as suicides from high buildings. The waves are mountains of water which tower to the heights of three-story buildings and the surfer shoots down these canyons of raging foam like an ant down a glass tower.

The surf in Southern California never gets that high or deadly. So, when the little rollers at Malibu begin to bore, the boys turn to Dana Point or Laguna Beach—where they come in through rocks—or Huntington Beach where they roll through pier pilings. A misstep and the result is a crackup that can put the Freeway to shame for mayhem, a course known as Blood Alley. Personal injury is scorned but a broken board is calamitous since the surfer is often short on money (because he won't work when the surf is running and sometimes when it isn't).

A new custom board costs $66 to $100 depending on whether they make their own or patronize the Stradivarii of surfboards, Hobie, Velzy, or Sweet.

Surfers' beaches are Indian camps where landlubbers can be detected by their haircuts and girls don't count. A surfer's idea of a date is two tickets to a surfing film. It is a young man's sport but a grandmother, Marge Calhoun, excels at it. It gives its practitioners a knot on their insteps, known as "surfers' bumps" from kneeling on boards and this sometimes means shoes cannot be worn over them—a matter of no concern to a surfer who feels he is dressed for the evening if he puts on a pair of zoris.

Some are impostors who lie on the beach and sun bathe and leave their boards stacked on the fence and get on them only in the back of the car for the ride home. But most of them are frenzied, dedicated, hooked addicts. They're a little nuts but glad of it. They have practiced their art since the days when boards were 100-pound hulls of solid wood. They risk pneumonia in winter because the swells are better. They feel sorry for *you* in that stuffy office.

Welcome to Golf

Of all the golf tournaments of the year, I guess my favorite is the Crosby. I guess it's because I enjoy watching people get shock treatment.

I don't know about you, but if there's one thing that discourages me about the game of golf it's to see a pro shoot a 62 from the back tees of a course I can't break 100 on. I could sit right down and have a good cry.

You see, the trouble with these pros is they don't really know how tough a game this is. I mean, they usually tee up in nice sunny weather with a slight breeze at their backs, the fairways hard, the greens medium fast and the crowd quiet and respectful. The guy who's putting well is the guy who wins but even the one who's putting poorly breaks 69.

The Crosby is something else. That's the tournament where they find out what a chamber of horrors 18 holes of golf can be. The clouds scud in low and gray. The wind turns your ears (and your language) purple. The cold makes your nose run and your eyes watery. The rain makes a swamp of the fairway.

The pros hate it. Every year one or more of them vows he'll never show up in that polar region again. And you know why? Because they have to play the game the way you and I play it.

Their fingers tremble from the frigid blasts. Yours and mine tremble on a 90-degree day. From fright. The wind is howling so fiercely, they suddenly notice the out-of-bounds markers. We notice them all the time. Even in dead calm.

Even Arnold Palmer leaves a few balls in the sand traps.

That's because they're full of water or melted snow and have the consistency of molasses. But, never mind. The point is he leaves them there just as we do all the time because our swing is a nervous spasm and it's nice to see Arnold Palmer find out what it's like. You feel like leaning over toward the television set and leering. "Aggravating, ain't it, Arnie? How do you like it, boy?"

The pros are used to getting on every hole in the circuit with a driver and a 9 iron. All of a sudden at the Crosby, par 5s are playing the way par 5 *ought* to play—the way they play for you and me, the way the Scots intended they should play when they invented the damn game.

They take clubs out of the bag they haven't had to use since they were kids. You see one of them off to the side of the green under a tree and you want to raise your glass of beer in a toast to the TV screen. "Terrible line to the pin from there, ain't it, Doug?" you sympathize. Then you mock: "That's the kind of shot I *always* have to the pin! Let's see you get *that* one down in two!"

The Crosby in adverse weather conditions is my favorite television show, Emmy Award stuff. You feel like doing a little dance when a ball bananas into the ocean—because you know the feeling so well. "Salt water ruins your ball," you warn the pro. "Also your score." You cheer when the winning score is announced—286. "What?" you jeer as the scoreboard comes in view with all the 299s and the 302s and 309 on it. "No 62s today, fellows? Come, come."

Even the winner pleases you—the old war horse, Doug Ford. You feel a pleasurable thrill as he comes on screen pacing like an uncaged panther. "Doug smells first money," you tell your wife. "He can't wait to get to that pay window."

You want Ford to win because, to tell the truth, his

swing isn't a helluva lot better than yours and mine—a lusty swipe, a hook-fighting trajectory. It's just as suited to snow-playing as it is to the sun-washed fast tracks and in the back of your mind you know Doug in his time has sunk many a putt through the snow—if the price was right.

It's even pleasing to hear the pros griping about the 10-handicap the baseball player Albie Pearson uses to win the $3000 pro-am. "Why, fellows," you find yourself saying to the screen. "We have that problem on the first tee on every round we play. You guys are just too used to teeing up with a field full of legit scratch players. You've got to learn how to watch yourselves on that first tee. That can often be more important than the 18th green."

I suppose, though, just because they had to wash out Sunday's play, they'll change the Crosby to a summer event. Our civilization veers away from everything with any character to it and substitutes something cheap or shoddy. I expect any day that a pre-fab golf course will be shipped around for all tournaments marked, MADE IN JAPAN, and a birdie guaranteed on every hole or your money back.

You have the feeling the Crosby in winter is golf as it was meant to be played. Perfection is monotonous. You get tired of the burlesque golf you otherwise see and you get a good feeling. You don't yell at the kids. You help with the dishes. You feel your own miserable game vindicated.

The only thing lacking is that nobody got poison ivy.

Fore Flusher

Myself, I can take golf or leave it alone.

But when I quit the magazine business my pals presented me with this real swinging pair of golf shoes and I was hooked. They're white kid with flaps hanging out like a dog's tongue and they have gold-plated cleats. They could almost shoot a 72 by themselves and they're not meant to be worn by anyone above a 2-handicap. If they are, they'll give you corns.

It's become my life's ambition to be able to wear them without both of us blushing. But I'm afraid my swing never will catch up to their elegance. Frankly, I have seen better form on a guy beating a carpet.

But there are other ways to earn your golden slippers if you're canny. To give you an idea, I played in a one-day tournament down at Hesperia the other day and shot a steady 103. Now, 103 may not sound like much to you, but when I tell you I did it in 56–47, you'll know you're not dealing with a nobody. I mean, just imagine Arnold Palmer shaving nine strokes from his front nine to his back nine and you have to remake the game.

It so happens I can tell him just how to do it.

I played at Hesperia with Hank Osborne, the newspaperman, and Bob Wilke, the movie bad guy. You'd know Bob if you saw him. He's the one who goes around shooting John Wayne in the back, selling guns to the Indians, and kidnaping the school marm off the stagecoach. He hits a golf ball so far, he considers a 250-yd. drive a shank.

I put the Murray method for lower scoring into effect

right on the first tee. When they ask, "What's your handicap?" you mumble or try to throw them off the scent by saying, "I'm nearsighted, my feet hurt, and I have this terrible memory for numbers." Above all, don't commit yourself till you know what handicap will be needed.

You play the first nine badly. In fact, you play both nines badly. The difference is, you *count* the first nine. Actually, you over-count. I mean, you get up on the green and start ticking off strokes on your fingers. You throw in one stroke you didn't even take and your partners—who will watch you carefully the first few holes because golfers don't trust each other, and with good reason—will protest, "You didn't have a ten. You only took a nine."

By the back nine, you will have established yourself as an overhonest goof who will never go anywhere in this dumb game. That's when you strike. You never see your partners from tee-to-green anyway; so always carry pocketsful of extra balls and when you come to an opening in the jungle, you nonchalantly drop a ball and stand there leaning on your club. When your partners come up, you observe casually, "I lie three here. I pushed my second shot into the rough." Actually, you only lie one there because you lost your tee shot and just walked the other ball up there.

I forgot to add, you never take a caddy—unless you happen to know he has a prison record. When you get in the hole, and mark your score, you say "I had a 5 there," then you look around, and if no one is looking at you funny, you frown and start to erase saying, "No that's not right, it was only a 4." This is known in golf as improving your lie. In other words, the first score was a lie, but the second was a better one.

Establishing your nearsightedness permits you to bend over and pick up your ball and squint at it even on the fairway. You explain, you just want to be sure it's yours. When you put it back down, of course, you tee it up on a tuft of grass you have kicked up with your cleats.

You don't have to tee your ball up in the rough. I have a better method. What you do in thick brambles is take out your 2-iron and take a whole flock of practice swings. When you have a clearing big enough to build a log cabin, you pretend to change your mind and go to a wood. A hostile caddy is very bad in this situation, too, because when you say "What's the club?" in the deep rough, he'll say "a scythe." "In that case," you say airily, "give me my 2-iron. But take the cover off the 4-wood. I'll be ready for it as soon as I take a few practice swings."

You have to be careful of the geometry. Don't wander so far off line that when you come back on the fairway, the most elemental triangulation will prove you couldn't have gotten where you are except by three 600-yard drives in a row. Always leave yourself in a position to explain sunnily if your partner looks suspicious, "A 1-iron. I hit it real good."

Actually, the only time I ever took out a 1-iron was to kill a tarantula. And I took a seven to do that. But I underclubbed. The shot was a brassie. But I only marked it on the card as a 5. And now I get to wear my new shoes to kill tarantulas.

Food Phils the Bill

I don't suppose there's anything he can do about it, but I see where the President's physical fitness program took another blow to the body (so to speak) this week.

I refer to a victory by Phil Rodgers in the L.A. Open. Phil, you may have noticed, is a young man built along the general contours of Minnesota Fats. If he gains ten more pounds and wins two more tournaments, he may force Vic Tanny to renovate his techniques—throw out all those barbells and put in chocolate eclairs.

His victory revives all the old arguments as to whether golfers are athletes or just outdoor pool sharks. He is, as it happens, only one of many touring pros whose waistlines disappeared years ago.

Later this month, Phil plays in the Lucky Lager Open at San Francisco but he probably should take on the Metracal Open—or vice versa—except that high-calorie golf seems to be the order of the day. In any other sport, Rodgers, Billy Casper, Bob Rosburg, Jack Nicklaus and Lionel Hebert would probably spend half their time in the steam room. Yet, Casper won the National Open, the Kentucky Derby of golf, Hebert and Rosburg won the PGA, and Nicklaus won the National Amateur twice.

All Phil Rodgers did was shoot a 62 Monday, a course and tournament record. It is significant, I think, that Mike Souchak whose silhouette was once the same side and front, took off 25 lb.—and staggered in with a hairy 77. He was only 4 strokes off when the day started; he was 19 when it ended. Rodgers got $7500; Mike got $155. If that doesn't bring back fudge and doughnuts, then someone mis-counted when he said there were 5,000,000 golfers in the country.

Whipped cream must also be good for the nerves. For Phil who, at age twenty-three, had every reason to come down with the ague overnight—this was the first time he had ever been leading a tournament after three rounds—rolled around Rancho on Monday as though it were a $2 Nassau. He looked from a distance as though he were too full to worry.

It was his skinny competitors who began to yip. Sou-chak, for instance, knocked $1000 over the fence at the funnel-like ninth hole when he blasted a wood out of bounds trying to overtake the front-running Rodgers who had cannily squeezed his 2-iron shot up to the green like toothpaste out of a tube.

If it was a baseball, the shortstop would have gloved it, because it never got more than three feet off the ground.

The central fact of Rodgers' incredible 9-stroke win was that it probably was no fluke. This stolid youngster is no stranger to birdie golf. He was tournament-tough at the age of nine when he won a trophy two inches taller than he was. He was throwing clubs at the age of four and a half.

He has either been on a golf course—or at a lunch counter —most of his life. He won so many junior championships, including the national, that he was a natural for a scholar-ship at the University of Houston, better known in the links world as the "University of Golf" where, the gag goes, the entrance requirements are a 64 on an accredited course and a sound short game.

Rodgers learned how to wrap woods and rap par. He won the National Collegiate. His biggest plus was his temperament. His only show of animation even in a pressure round is an occasional burp.

As if he didn't have enough going for him, Phil had a caddy who was an equally confident young man. Billy Bishop is a twenty-three-year-old Negro fashion plate in jodhpurs, Ivy pants and leather cap who saw nothing remarkable in Phil's sixty-two since, after all, as he pointed out, he clubbed Rodgers on every shot all the way around including a ninety-foot putt.

Now, most people sink ninety-foot putts with their eyes closed and their breaths held but Billy had the line all the way. "It broke both ways, so I told him to play it straight," Billy observed with the air of a man who would have been surprised if it didn't go in.

A songwriter when he isn't breaking par, Billy's main apprehension was what his cut would be of Phil's $7500. Billy needs the money because, as he puts it, he "resigned from the post office," which leaves just another problem for the President to wrestle with.

For Billy, the real suspense of the round took place after it was over, because he recalls advising Don January to put away his 7-iron and take an 8 on one hole at Palm Springs last year. Don did—and sank a hole-in-one for $50,000. Billy got only $300 of it, Billy says, and Billy has been wondering ever since if he did the right thing in quitting the post office. He was particularly apprehensive when the other caddies kept joshing him he was going to be "paid off in the dark" or "under the bridge," caddy-ese for short-changed. But Billy got his $750. The day was a triumph for food and faith all around.

Meanwhile, hand over that milkshake, will you? I'm trying to break a hundred.

A Toast to Eddie

If I were a horse today, I'd be tempted to throw a party —champagne, fillies, barn dancing, all kinds of horsing around.

You see, George Edward Arcaro, the well-known bongo drummer and horseback rider, has decided to hang up his tack. To understand what this can mean to a horse, just imagine the feelings of the crew of the *Bounty* when they put Captain Bligh to sea in that lifeboat, or the Russians when they got word Stalin was running a temperature.

There are two ways to win horse races—by guile or by terror. Eddie Arcaro chose the knout. His riding style, as far as the horse was concerned, was early Cossack, a combination of Genghis Khan, Attila the Hun, and Jack the Ripper in goggles and silks. The horse was running not for his oats but for his life because he knew the quicker he got to the finish line, the quicker he could start to heal. There might have been times when the trainer or the stable wasn't trying. But there never was a time when G. Edward Arcaro wasn't. There were times, in fact, when the horse seemed superfluous.

Eddie Arcaro never actually carried a dying-run horse across the finish line but he was straining so hard his nose frequently made the photo in a dead heat with the horse's. The Arcaro nose, inadequately described as "banana," was as fine a utensil for sniffing out rancid horseflesh as for good steaks. A jockey's secret of winning is usually the simple: "Stay off bad horses." But the Arcaro method was such that even bad horses extended themselves—like deer fleeing a fire.

It is well-established that fear makes supermen of tabby cats, something to do with adrenalin. I don't even know whether a horse has adrenalin. Neither did Eddie Arcaro. But he did know that when they ran scared, they ran faster. He set out to make himself the Dracula of the homestretch. He steered 4779 terror-stricken horses into the winner's circle in his time for a gross take of $30,039,543.

It wasn't only the horses Signor Arcaro terrified. It was also the other riders. A man with the nice gentle disposition of a bear with cubs—or ulcers—Eddie's riding tactics were right out of the Mafia. He took the position that whatever he couldn't run past, he could run through. Impartial observers say his technique for snatching saddle-cloths showed that pickpocketing lost a first-rate prospect when someone hoisted Arcaro into a saddle.

He knocked so many riders in the infield in the early days that there wasn't a boy in the tack room who would dare let Eddie Arcaro get outside him. As a result, he was on the ground every other month which had the effect of keeping his weight down since it is commonly known that the simplest way to keep the weight down is not to eat and the simplest way not to eat is not to be able to afford it. Eddie spent one whole year on foot in 1942 for trying to deliver a rider, Vincenzo Nodarse, to his Maker prematurely, by way of the infield. What happened in the Cowdin Stakes that year was that Nodarse (pronounced "Nodarcy") almost became No-dicey when he came over on Arcaro leaving the gate. Arcaro, with blood in his eye, gave chase and drew alongside. "No! No! Eddie! No mean it!" cried Nodarse. "Neither do I," Eddie told him as Nodarse went through the rail.

Eddie won five Kentucky Derbies but he won 4774 other races because he rode every race as though it were a Kentucky Derby—or as though a lynch mob were after him. It's an axiom around the track that a good rider cannot make a bad horse good but a bad rider can make a good horse bad. Arcaro was the good rider who frequently made bad horses good—or good and scared. In late years, he learned to control his temper. But he never let the horses know it.

He didn't always win races like a fullback on horseback. Sometimes he snatched them like a cut-purse, other times like a card shark. His theory was that 90 percent of thoroughbred horses didn't give a damn whether they won or not—and maybe 10 percent of the jockeys. This percentage leeway gave E. Arcaro plenty of room to become the top race rider of his day. He never took the safe way home but he sometimes took the sneaky way. He won the Manhattan Stakes once with a sprinter in 2:36½. Most horses can walk faster than that but Eddie slickered the routers by pretending his horse was all out to stay in front, a tactic which would never work with Arcaro who had a built-in clock in his own brain.

Born the son of a fruit-peddler in Cincinnati, Arcaro was never a born rider, except on the back of streetcars. But he was a born competitor. The famous story about him recounted by Roger Kahn concerns the trainer who first watched him scrambling all over a horse's back at Caliente. "You'll kill yourself," the trainer told him coldly. "If you can make a rider, I can make a watch." Arcaro said nothing but continued to accept mounts. Later, after he had won cups and a stable contract, he turned to the trainer innocently and said "OK, now let's see you make a watch."

I got a better idea. Let's see them make another Eddie Arcaro.

Point Is Serenity

Judo, as almost everyone in the world knows by now, is a generic name given to a group of Japanese combat and self-defense techniques ranging in scope from a simple form of arm-wrestling to an exotic art of wooden sword fighting.

To its practitioners, it is more than a sport. It is a semi-religion as ceremonial as being presented at court. Its purpose is not to defeat but "to attain a sense of inner security and serenity"—the conquest, as it were, of inner space. Just after you have been slammed to the ground in front of a crowd, you are expected to stand at attention and bow gravely to your opponent as if he had just handed you a plate of fortune cookies and tea.

The dedicated "Judoka" closes his eyes and shudders when some crass beginner demands to know whether a Judo champion can lick Argentine Rocca or Sonny Liston because he regards such a question as about on a vulgar plane with a query as to whether Billy Graham can lick Bishop Sheen.

Nevertheless, the judo world was shocked last month when the judo championship of the world went over to a young Dutch upstart, some rotter from Rotterdam who dethroned the Japanese from a sport which has been traditionally theirs for centuries.

I knew the development would rock devotees from the Sawtelle Dojo to the Emperor's Palace. So I invited the editors of *Black Belt* out to the house for a discussion. In judo, a black belt is a badge of merit entitled to be worn over the bedsheet only by those most proficient in the art, men (or women) who have littered the mats of the world with the vertebrae of the most opponents.

Publisher Edmund Jung, and editor George Asawa brought with them Koichi Tohei and Hidetaka Nishiyama and after we had bowed and hissed greetings, it was explained that Tohei's specialty was an abstruse martial art called "Aikido," while Nishiyama was one of the world's foremost tile-shatterers, an expert in "Karate."

None of them was particularly moved by Japan's loss in judo. "Is not point," Tohei assured me sincerely. "Point is serenity, not combat. Is necessary to make mind like calm surface of pond so moon can refrect in it. Prease observe."

And he closed his eyes and poked a pudgy forefinger into his abdomen about two inches below the navel. "Is what we call one-point. Is center of gravity. One imposes serenity by trying to bring mind below navel. I will now exhale breath and imagine breath going from top of skull down through spinal cord, ending in one-point down here."

There was a sound through the room like air going out of a tire. Tohei's face lost its ruddiness, turned gray, then white. He seemed to stop breathing all together. Then, his eyes shot open. They were merry. He giggled.

"Is what we call the 'ki.' Is the breath of life. In Aikido, men sit for hours in the snow and at end of the time skin still warm. Mind must control body. In self-defense, mind make other man do what you want. See!"

He invited Asawa to attack. I looked apprehensively toward the piano but Tohei neatly dodged the rush and tied Asawa into a bowknot. "Mind control body and opponent's body," he explained. "Reason simple: when inhale, not strong. When exhale, strong."

"Do you have two chairs?" Asawa asked. He placed them a yard apart, lay down with his feet on one and his head on the other. "Sit on my stomach," he ordered. "I weigh 205," I protested. "No matter," he said. I sat down gingerly, I expected his form to become a V abruptly. It didn't. "See!" exclaimed Tohei. "Mind very powerful. Put arm out, close eyes and think of water flowing from brain out arm and one will be unable to bend it."

I closed my eyes. I extended my arm. I thought of water flowing out. Asawa seized it. "Ow!" I hollered. My arm collapsed into a swastika. "You must concentrate," Tohei told me reproachfully. "See! Can make heart beat faster. Watch pulse."

He closed his eyes. I counted his pulse. It leaped twenty beats a minute. "I can do that," I told him. "I just take a shot of brandy."

"In karate," Nishiyama told me, "object is to achieve speed and dexterity, not maim. Must learn to pull punch, otherwise harm opponent. Have to have faith in opponent." "We have the same thing," I told him. "We call it 'wrestling.'"

After they had left, I got to thinking about it. I crouched in a corner, closed my eyes and began to exhale. My wife came in. "I thought the boiler was leaking," she said crossly. "What on earth are you doing? Your face is turning blue."

"I'm trying to get at one-point with my 'ki,'" I told her. "Getting my mind down below my navel."

She gave me a look. "For that, you have to squat in a corner?" she asked. "Besides," she said, "if you get any fatter, you won't have any navel." She flounced out of the room. "I'll buy you a kimono," she said. "And by the way, rotsa ruck."

Last of the Borgias

The Last of the Borgias would be a terrible disappointment to students of medieval history. He is short, bald, cheerful, and his eyes twinkle with mischief, not murder.

The worst he can do to you is call a two-shot foul. He has no poison cup, and the chances are he wouldn't even pull the wings off a butterfly. Lucrezia would be ashamed of him.

But Sid Borgia, or Santa Borgia, as he was christened when he was the first-born son of an Italian coal miner in West Virginia, has a distinction of his own. He's the oldest in point of service and the best from any point of the officials in the National Basketball Assn. As long as there's been an NBA on the boards, there's been a Sid Borgia.

Sid never played high school or college basketball for the simple reason he never went to high school or college. In fact, he didn't linger in grammar school long. Raised in the pit of the Depression when the family moved from West Virginia to New York City which, in that economic holocaust, was just West Virginia with subways, he sold papers and went to work for a living as soon as he outgrew the baby carriage.

Sid has always been a willing worker and people have been willing to let him work. He was drafted in the Army almost before Roosevelt's signature was dry on the draft bill and slogged around for four years in the South Pacific and came back as a skilled bullet dodger and not much else. He tried baseball umpiring for a time in Class D when he was offered a tryout in the newly formed pro basketball loop. "But I've never even done college basketball!" Sid warned them. "Good," they told him. "You won't have any bad habits."

Pro basketball in the 40s was a whistle-stop, dirty-shirt routine which took one to all the glamour spots of the U.S. —Sheboygan, Waterloo, Iowa, Anderson, Indiana, the Tri-Cities, Providence. One year, they had seventeen cities in the loop and would have let in as many more who could pay for their own basketballs. Sid struggled around to all of them.

You got $40 a game and all you could eat. You took the train everywhere and slept sitting up because the budget didn't include luxuries like beds.

You got to Waterloo, Iowa, on time only if a certain cab driver who was a basketball nut was on duty. No non-fan would take on the twenty-four-mile loop.

Sid sometimes hitch-hiked to games. Sometimes you had to phone ahead to be sure the franchise hadn't folded, but Sid Borgia never lost faith in pro basketball, not even when he took pay cuts at a time the economy was going the other way. Like most other heads of families riding this leaky league in the early days, he had to take other jobs. But he always saw to it they didn't interfere with basketball.

Like most of the officials in the league, Sid comes about to a center's belt buckle. There is a reason for this: Sid, now the supervisor of referees, picks new ones for ability to run, not see over transoms.

A basketball official gets more abuse than any other official. This is because the fan is closer. No dugout shields the players' taunts and when the crowd hears the coach storming "Where's the foul, Sid?" it takes up the chant.

Sid thinks this is good. He has seen basketball grow, fall back, come on again, and he is proud of the part he had to play in it. He thinks the twenty-four-second rule, even though it means he and his partner have to gallop six miles a night up and down the floor, is the greatest thing since Dr. Naismith. "The savior of the game," insists Sid. "It did away with the late-game deliberate foul which was the most sickening thing you had to contend with and was killing the game."

He finds the biggest difficulty in recruiting new officials is they think they should throw away their whistles when they come in the pros. "I can take a whistle blower and taper him off. But if he doesn't blow it, I can't say 'Blow it, dammit!'"

Basketball is so sensitive to scandal, referees sneak into town every way but in dark glasses and beards. They cannot stay at the same hotel or travel on the same plane as a team. They recognize the unequal power they have. "Ninety percent of the calls are judgment calls," admits Sid. "You have to have men of unquestioned integrity."

He thinks the success of the sport in L.A. was critical. He even remembers when he saw it come. For five months, fans had sat in silence at this strange new sport in L.A. until one night in the playoffs in a tie game and a close call, Borgia saw a fan stir in the back of the net. "Borgia," he shouted. "You're a creep!"

It made Sid feel good all over. After seventeen years, he knew the mating call of the fan when he heard it.

Call of the Surf

Something new has been added to our family. It's all blue on the outside and soft and white and marshmallowy on the inside and it gets the best of tender, loving care.

It's a surfboard.

For those of you unfamiliar with the implement, a surfboard is a sea-going piece of foam plastic in the shape of a shark with a keel on the back and a boy on top.

The boy, like the board, looks like something that has escaped from an aquarium. His hair is so long and full of sea-life it looks like a kelp bed. His body is burned melba, his eyes are red-rimmed and sun-faded, his nose is peeled down to the cartilage and he has dromedary-sized bumps on his insteps from kneeling on his board and praying for trouble.

This is the genus Surfer, the illogical biological successor to the Muscle Head of Muscle Beach of the Thirties, the Drug Store Cowboy of the Twenties and the bicycle-batty Scorcher of an earlier, more-innocent, inland era. The teen-ager of the Sixties has put to sea.

The sport of surfboarding probably was first practiced by some panicky Polynesian who boarded a piece of driftwood to avoid feeding a pack of hungry cannibals or marrying a cockeyed hula dancer.

Only a handful of mainlanders picked up the sport until recently, probably because the original plank boards were big enough to be launched with champagne across the bow and heavy enough to require running lights in a crowded harbor.

The revolution in plastics revolutionized the sport and produced a board so light the day may come when it can be floated down to the water on the end of a string like a kite. But it is like a woman: it only looks soft. Australian lifeguards liked to have died laughing when they saw their first one and predicted you could pick your teeth with what was left of it after the first Pacific chop. But today the sport is booming there, in South Africa and South America. Teams of enthusiasts are combing the coasts of Europe and the Mediterranean for shooting surfaces.

It is the fastest-growing sport in the world considering it began with two Borneans trying to shoot a shower of spears and today the Southern California tidelands have more surfers than sharks, an imbalance the sharks do their best to remedy from time to time.

The surfers not only have the sea, sharks, traffic and the truant officers to battle, they have the public and politics. A surfboard keel, or "skeg," goes through shallow water like a submerged guillotine and the "red tide" on a surfers' beach doesn't always mean plankton in the water. The boom in surfboarding has produced a surge in sutures and skin grafts, to say nothing of eye patches and bone splints.

The flatlanders who tumble to the sea with their beach umbrellas and pickle jars on a Sunday afternoon take a dim view of their kids' legs coming back to them in filets and the skirmishing has been physical on the more populated beaches. The incidents usually come out in the papers as "Surfers Riot at Redondo." Or Malibu. Or Rincon.

County lifeguards have tried to meet the problem by earmarking certain beaches for surfers only, but once the taxpayer has gotten the playpen assembled under the umbrella and the Saran Wrap off the potato salad, he's prepared to fight it out on that line if it takes all day, and the feud is on.

When surfers break out big buttons urging "Pray for Surf!" the flatlanders counter with their version "Pray for Sharks!"

Surfers come in all shapes and sizes. Little ones who never comb their hair and are so water-logged their skin is turning to scales are known as "Gremmies." The class of surfers whose boards are stacked on arrival at the beach and never get wet unless it rains on the way home are known as "Hodaddies." A "Hodaddy" is a poser and even if he does enter the water, he goofs up the wave and suddenly the foam is alive with churning surfboards, skegs gleaming like meat-axes in the sun.

Surfboards are turned out like violins to fit the characteristics of the soloist and orders are running three weeks behind. Kids can make them in the backyard if the family doesn't mind being hip deep in resin and fibre-cloth.

As a sport, it will have to be measured for form and style like figure-skating. It has its Mickey Mantles and Maury Willses. They run to two types: "hotdoggers" who dance up and down the boards like guys in the midst of a hot foot; and "stoics," the lordly, contemptuous types who master the raging sea and board like a motionless matador frustrates a mad bull.

You are expected to tempt danger by continually steering your ride into the mouth of the beast, the most precarious part of the wave, and then getting out of it still on deck and not on the floor of the ocean.

In high surf in Hawaii, it rivals skiing for peril. And there is no equivalent to the snow patrol. The surf patrol is apt to have fins and sharp teeth and to mistake the snowy surfboards for sea-going popsicles. Surfing through rocks and trestles is considered more fun even than surfing through people.

It has its own lexicon:

"Walking the Nose" means just that. Roaming around on the foredeck while the board is careening along a steep wave.

"Five Toes Over the Nose"—a feat comparable to hitting five-for-five, wrapping your toes around the front of the board. A variation is "Three Toes Over the Nose," which starts out the same as the five-toed stunt—and then a runaway skeg comes by.

"Taking the Soup"—riding all the way into the shore foam.

It's a fraternity you can join only three hundred yards or more offshore, a minority without rights, a fact which makes Lifeguard Lieutenant Bob Burnside in residency at Surfrider Beach, Malibu, thoughtful:

"To some, the term 'surfer' means a salt-water loafer," Bob admits. "When the day is hot and the surf is flat, they can cause trouble like any bored kids. But, man, when the surf is up, the surfer couldn't care less about booze, broads, money, war or food. All he wants is surf. He'll go over property, step on anything or anybody to get on that ocean. It's a problem. But it's a better problem than figuring out what to do with them hanging around alleys."

Fat Man of Pool

The fat man drummed his fingers on the table and his eyes darted around the room. Ordinarily, Rudolph Walter Wanderone wouldn't spot a person he didn't know because everyone from Dog Walk to the north to Crab Orchard on the south of Du Quoin, Illinois, knows the Fat Man.

You'd know him, too, if he looked more like Jackie Glea-
son from the neck up. Right? The Hustler from the movie
of the same name. Minnesota Fats, alias New York Fats.

Fats is restless because this is race week in Du Quoin.
And there might be some "marks"—people looking to give
their money away to strangers—out there in that crowd.
Fats spends his life looking for marks.

He goes through the world carrying a pool cue in one
hand and a deck of cards in one pocket. The cards have
eyes in the back of them. The pool cue is 58 inches long
and 20 ounces heavy. It's collapsible and as delicately bal-
anced as a micrometer. For Fats, it's his equalizer.

You wouldn't think Dowell, Illinois, which is only a
three-cornered shot from Du Quoin, would produce the
world's best in anything—unless maybe hog calling. There
aren't enough people in it for one good bridge tournament.
But Fats was the world's best pool hustler in his day. He
passed through towns like a gray shadow. He hustled the
best. His life was a click of cue balls and a silent passing
of money.

He was a silhouette you could duplicate only with a lifetime supply of plover's eggs and champagne. And it robbed
him of the hustler's main stock in trade—anonymity. Pretty
soon he was as well known in the pool halls as a brass spit-
toon. Hustlers he never heard of used to practice nights for
the day when they would run into the Fat Man. They came
into town looking for him and the Fat Man finally got to the
point he could sit like a toad in a second story pool hall in
Chicago and wait for them.

"Everybody wants a piece of the Fat Man," the grifters admitted. Fats was a world's champion at a shadowy sport
that symbolized to a nation a misspent youth and a squandered adulthood. Fats could do tricks with a pool cue

Willie Hoppe would have gotten invited to the White House for. Willie Mosconi could put on a white tie and monkey suit and go on the Ed Sullivan Show. But the Fat Man just shuffled around in blue slacks and light-tan shoes. He put a tie on only when he went to Johnson City for the tournament, the one-pocket grift—the summit of hustlery.

The Fat Man goes through life via side entrances. A hustler doesn't want his picture on national TV any more than he wants it in the post office. The Fat Man's calling card is a 55-inch waist and a pool stroke that's pure silk. He doesn't ask anything of life but that he shouldn't have a rail shot when all the money is on the line and the "mark" is on, having a run of luck.

He has played in all the lonely sections of town where the pool halls are. He has seen the sun come up redly through drawn blinds at the end of 50 hours of steady pool, a stubble of beard on his cheeks, his lips cracked and dry but his wrist as sure and steady as a piston.

Fats doesn't drink becaue you can't drink and shoot hustler's pool. You give the "mark" a break with every beaker of booze you throw down. Sometimes in three and four-day matches, the Fat Man would watch with satisfaction as the other fellow hurried to the bar for a quick one to recharge the batteries. "I know three, maybe four, people in the world can shoot and drink," he says. "No more."

Fats is forty-nine now and out of stroke, as the hustlers say when the balls don't drop. He's had to play so many guys one-handed the cue feels strange with 10 fingers on it. He tried to quit, went into retirement. He married a girl from Dowell and came down to sit in the sun and pick up stray dogs.

The Fat Man loves animals. He has more dogs and cats in his backyard than the rest of Dowell put together. When they smell a skunk, the whole neighborhood gets an earache. He bums bones from butchers for them and he hustles for stray dogs. Friends swear if Fats saw a fly with a broken leg he'd put a sling on it. He'd let a rabid dog bite him.

Fats blew the biggest hustle in the world when he didn't capitalize on the movie when it was up for Academy Award. He could have been on every show on television if anyone could find him. Instead, he sat on the porch and fed the dogs. "I'm the laziest guy in the world," he admits. Someone sued the movie company for him and Fats brightens at the prospect of a little fresh money but is bored at the prospect of having to testify to anything.

"I don't do nuthin'," he admits. "I went on television over to Harrisburg once." He also lectured on the art of bank pool at the University of Indiana.

He's proud that he came from a long line of educators and professional people. The Wanderones were German-Swiss and produced several college professors and doctors—but only one hustler, Fats. "But I was the best in the world at what I done," he says quietly. That is something not many men can say with any assurance.

The grifters in a pool hall are a cynical bunch—about everything but their own legends. The Fat Man is their legend. The game of pool died when someone saw the drama in the legend of the Fat Man who could make a pool cue talk and hustlers cry.

Fats is a familiar sight on the streets of Du Quoin during Hambletonian week. Fresh money is arriving in town with every rented car and Fats is trying to divert it to his ample pockets. He comes into town maybe three, four times a day, going home only to feed the dogs or let the cats out.

His pretty wife chats with the customers and their wives

up front, but Fats is in another part of town where the curtains are drawn, a light bulb blinks under a green eyeshade, the cards are dealt and the hustle is on. The pool cue is in the trunk of the car, just in case. "I don't miss no place," says Fats. "I like wherever I'm at. But when I'm gone, I don't miss it." His home has got green felt on it and pockets in all the corners and chalk on the rail.

As Fats says, he's one of a kind. And probably the last of his kind. Minnesota Fats. New York Fats. Illinois Fats. American Fats—Vanishing American Fats.

Keep to the Left

The only thing I know for sure about a car is that the clock doesn't work one month after you buy it. Sometimes the rest of it doesn't, either.

Actually, the real reason I came back here to cover the Indianapolis 500 is I'm crazy about noise. Besides, I'm told the race is almost as exciting as the freeway interchange at rush hour. The only thing is the drivers don't swear at each other.

It's not so much a sporting event as a death watch. They hold it, fittingly, on Memorial Day. It has long since tied the one-day extermination record set by the German Luftwaffe in Poland in 1939, and since tied by many including the Red Army in Budapest a couple of years ago. They should start the race with "Taps."

It's all in the interests of research. How else could you prove 170 m.p.h. is too fast to take a curve? Personally, I would take that on the manufacturer's or the National

Safety Council's say-so but some people have to be shown. This race has made believers out of about four dozen drivers in its time. But since they all left the track with a sheet over their faces, they couldn't pass their accumulated knowledge on to posterity. It wouldn't do any good, anyway. If anyone ever paid any attention to auto fatality records we would have gone back to the horse and surrey long ago.

The biggest suckers at Indianapolis are not the drivers but the owners. Would you believe it, these guys pay upwards of one hundred grand for a car to enter in this thing? And what cars! Honest John must drool when he thinks of customers like this. If you or I got one of these lemons off the lot, we would call the Better Business Bureau before we got them home. These things not only don't have any back-up lights, they don't even back up.

You have to *push* them to get started. I have bought a lot of cars like that in my time but not at one hundred grand. No radio, heater, ashtrays, glove compartment. You get—now, get this—about three miles to the gallon if you're lucky. I mean, you have to tow your own gas station around with you just to go to the beach.

You know what the only safety feature is? A roll-bar. So help me. The brakes wouldn't stop a scooter. God help you if you need them in a hurry. Actually, if you want to stop by 10 o'clock, you start braking at 8:15.

The wife won't care for the interior. Not even new seat covers would help. The windshield wipers don't work. In fact, there aren't any. You can't put the top up in the rain— no top.

The car is tipped so far to the left (the race is counterclockwise) the only way to go right is to roll over.

It's hard on tires, uses oil, and wait till you hear the

muffler. You'd get a ticket just pushing it through Beverly Hills, it's so noisy. Actually, you don't see an Indianapolis race, you hear it. You get a punctured ear-drum just flying over it.

The paint jobs would make you cover your eyes. They got things like "The Joe Bfspltk Bore and Stroke Special" splattered on them. They're not cars, they're 400-h.p. billboards.

Nevertheless, the guys in them get all the best of it. There are thirty-three of the best drivers in the world on the track. None of them has been drinking. All have their operator's licenses. The traffic jams are at least moving. Nothing is so hard on the blood pressure as sitting still in one. And there are no trucks.

I think the competition is unrealistic. To get more in line with the genuine automotive facts of life I would recommend a medley of events for Memorial Day.

For instance, I would like to see a couple of laps—if the cars last that long—run by drivers who have just picked up their cars right off a used car lot. Preferably from a guy who slaps fenders on a TV commercial.

Now, this would add a lot of suspense to the race. Because you wouldn't know which of these cars had sugar in the gas tanks or sawdust in the transmission. Then there would be the one with the brake drums scored.

The fellow who bought the car which had belonged to two little old ladies from Pasadena who only used it to go to church would probably hit the first turn before he found out the frame was sprung from too many accidents. As he would hit the wall, he would notice the black leather jacket shreds from the former owner this happened to.

The "one-owner" car would be interesting when some drivers found out the "one-owner" was a near-sighted alcoholic who drove the car into a swimming pool on several occasions.

Then there would be the "New Year's Eve Special" event in which all contestants would fill up on champagne and sleeping pills and then go out on the track at full throttle. To give reality to it, I would recommend again that one-half of the field go clockwise and the other counter.

There would be a race in which five of the drivers would be women who would signal for a left turn and then go right, a race where you would drive down the straightaway not knowing at which point some woman would back down a driveway into you.

There would be a lap or two in which part of the field were behind in their payments but up on their insurance and half-inclined to close the gap.

We would have drivers in the field from states where they had two-lane highways and the only pedestrians were cows. We would have traffic light races where half the field was color-blind.

We would have pedestrians crossing the tracks at intervals to give some life to the race. Also some death. We would have races where the guy behind you honked his horn constantly and kept pointing to your rear tire even though nothing was wrong with it.

We would have races with motorcycle cops hiding behind billboards and races in the dark where your tires got flat and you didn't have any flares, flashlights or funds to call the auto club.

We would have races with cars actually owned by two little old ladies from Pasadena and motors thus too sluggish to pass trucks on a curve with another car coming.

We would have races where your wife would keep saying "Are you sure this is the right way, dear?" or where you never knew when the baby in the back was going to conk you with a rattle.

We would have a race where you had something to think about besides turning left for five hundred miles, posted zones and school crossings and off-ramps designed by guys who got their start in Chinese puzzles. It wouldn't be Indianapolis, but it would be a lot closer to home, and no less deadly.

"Ladies and gentlemen, we interrupt this program to take you to the Indianapolis 500 raceway for a special broadcast. Take it away, Indianapolis . . ."

"Good afternoon (*b-r-r-zoom, b-r-r-zip*), racing fans everywhere. This is your friendly old racecaster—Oh, just a minute, here comes one—(*b-r-r-zip, b-r-r-zoom*)—Windy Whitesock bringing all the thrills and spills of Indianapolis on race week. And we have with us one of the most famous drivers of them all, Leadfoot Lonigan. Good afternoon, Leadfoot. I guess you got your nickname from a habit of tromping down on the old accelerator, eh?"

Leadfoot: "Well, no. I got this here lead foot, you see you can feel it right there. I lost my real one in Langhorne ten years ago."

Windy: "Oh, er. Well, I guess that must help your driving, eh?"

Leadfoot: "Only until you have to stop, Windy. But it's real good for getting out of bed in the morning. I mean, the old lady yells up 'Get the lead out,' and I throw my foot over the side and, believe me, the rest of you follows. The only thing is, you come through the ceiling if you're not careful."

Windy: "Heh, heh. Well, Leadfoot, guess this year's field is going to be one of the toughest, eh?"

Leadfoot: "Tough? Lissen, there isn't a piece of iron out there that belongs out of a junk yard. I could qualify for this thing reading a book. If I could read, that is. They ought to make me run on three wheels just to make it fair. We had some great drivers in the old days but these guys couldn't make a left turn on a crowded intersection. No, back when I was a kid we had 'Fireball' Finnegan, 'Yellow Light' Harrigan, and 'Cartwheel' Clancy."

Windy: "Those were drivers, eh? Tell me, how did they come by those colorful nicknames? Just picked 'em up, eh?"

Leadfoot: "Well, 'Fireball' got his because the last time we saw him, that's just what he was. He was just an ash when we got to him. They sent an ambulance out but all they needed was an ash tray. 'Yellow Light' Harrigan was a guy who spun out so much back in 1950 that they had the yellow light on all through the race. Took them three days to complete it. Old 'Yellow Light' had a poor sense of direction. Kept thinking he ought to go right and had to stop and check his road map all the time.

" 'Cartwheel' was just a guy who went out in his bathrobe and slippers on race morning and got caught in traffic and the next thing we knew he was in the race. He holds all lap records for cartwheeling through the straightaway. He was disqualified because the rules state airborne records don't count but if he had flipped one more time he could have qualified for the Cleveland air races. Then, there was Smokey White . . ."

Windy: "Who was Smokey White?"

Leadfoot: "Smokey was a guy who liked to navigate by keeping one eye on the smoke curling out of the smokestack behind the straightaway. Turned out he only had one eye. That was the year the field finished on top of old Smokey. Literally."

"Windy: "They have widened the tires this year, Lead-foot. Are there any other modifications you might suggest?"

Leadfoot: "Yeah. They ought to widen the front seats so you could take 'em to a drive-in movie. And there ought to be a cigarette lighter."

Windy: "Do you like alcohol injection?"

Leadfoot: "Hell, no, I'd rather drink it straight."

Windy: "Do you ever have nightmares?"

Leadfoot: "You bet I do. I dream I'm a spectator at one of these things. Just imagine. No crash helmet, goggles, flameproof suit. No armor around you. No insurance. It's written right in my policy it's void if I even listen to one of these things on the radio. I wouldn't be anywhere but on the track on race day. Those 250,000 daredevils in the infield and stands scare me to death. I mean, don't they *care* anything at all about their wives and families? They're nuts is what they are, just plain nuts. I'd rather walk wings with a hangover than be looking over the rail in this race. And now if you'll excuse me, I have to go and get my leg buffed."

THE GRAND OLD GAME

Voice of the Turtles

Spring is a time of year when the ground thaws, trees bud, the income tax falls due—and everybody wins the pennant.

Baseball is a game where a curve is an optical illusion, a screwball can be a pitch or a person, stealing is legal and you can spit anywhere you like except in the umpire's eye or on the ball.

Spring and baseball are perfect for each other.

A slight fever seizes everyone, hopes and blood pressure get high, splay-footed outfielders begin to look like Kiki Cuyler, overanxious rookies remind you that Babe Ruth was an overanxious rookie, too, and perfect strangers come up to you and ask what ever happened to the bunt and the hit-and-run.

But nowhere is the union between the game and the season better exemplified than in the manager's springtime quote. This is a bit of nonsense that rolls around as regularly as April Fool's and is about as credible, the real voice of the turtle. Anyone who believes a manager's springtime quote gets a lifetime supply of fortune cookies to play the stock market with and a card that entitles him to buy the Brooklyn Bridge wholesale.

It's not the manager's intent to deceive himself or the front-office. It's the customers he's trying to get to bite at a bad pitch. In his heart, he knows down to the last decimal point what his team is capable of. The idea is to keep the fans or the press from knowing it. The watchword must be unbridled optimism. The season ticket sale must be protected even if it spoils your appetite just to talk about the team.

There are several handy euphemisms which can be called into service to conceal the athletic bankruptcy you are bringing home from training camp. Here are some of the most common, followed by their real meanings:

"We're going back to sound fundamental baseball." No hitters.

"We're basically a power club." No pitchers.

"We'll surprise a lot of people." Especially the owner when he finds we have no hitters or pitchers and can't run very well, either.

"This club could go all the way." Oh, brother! So could a rock in water.

"We're taking 'em as they come." We're in a slump.

"We'll be up for this one." The guys got to bed for a change.

"We're not afraid of anybody." That's right. We're afraid of *everybody*.

"These guys pull their pants on one at a time, same as we do." We're in for a slaughtering.

"We won't be afraid to take chances." What else can we do?

"We'll play percentages." We'll be afraid to take chances.

"This is a well-balanced league." Or, put another way, I don't see how any of them can win it. The only well-balanced league in baseball is the New York Yankees.

"He's got a big league arm." At the dinner table. On the

field you can't trust him to *hand* the ball to the cutoff man.

"The greatest catching prospect since Gabby Hartnett." Forgive me, Gabby. The only thing this guy can do as well as you is talk.

"He's got to come up with a new pitch to take it all." He's got to come up with a new arm just to stay on the club.

"My big guy could break Maris' record." For strikeouts. As for the other, he couldn't hit sixty-one fair pop flies in a season if his mother was pitching.

"Our bonus kid should benefit from a year's experience." Yeah. Now he *knows* he can't hit a curve ball. Last year he only suspected it. The only reason I play him is the front office is embarrassed. They paid two hundred grand for this kid and the stockholders scream if we don't put him to work. I wish they had him picking up cigar butts instead of lousing up my lineup.

"These are grown men and we're going to treat them as such." Even the private eyes gave up and got loaded. The only way to tail these guys is at a stagger.

"The potential is there." We have the makings of the world's finest floating crap game.

"We're not conceding anything to anybody." Ha!

"We'll be pulling all the stops." I can't look.

"We're ready right now for the bell." Help!

Game of Numbers

I think it was Mark Twain who first said, "What do you want—the truth or statistics?" If he didn't, he should have.

I say that because it seems to me of late that the game of statistics has begun to run away with the game of baseball. I mean, it's not a sport any more, it's a multiplication table with base lines. You don't need writers to cover it, you need certified public accountants. I expect the World Series to be played any year now between two squads of adding machines.

There are even players whose statistics make them larger than life-sized and they become public monuments rather than members of a team. I refer you to the nonsense of a year ago when Stan Musial got his 2000th hit—or his 500th double, or whatever it was.

You would have thought the Cardinals clinched the World Series. They immediately stopped the game, managers, rival players, coaches and even umpires hurried out to shake Stan's hand. He left the game at once so he could catch a plane for the Ed Sullivan Show or Kukla, Fran and Ollie, or the White House or all three. No one remembers who won the game. It didn't matter. That's the point.

I remember driving through St. Louis last September and I happened to hear a Stan Musial press conference. He was announcing he was going to play another season. There were all kinds of reasons: he needed a certain number of hits to break somebody-or-other's old record; he needed X-number of doubles to pass somebody else's record. Way down at the bottom of the list of things he wanted to do was help the Cardinals win a pennant. I was surprised he thought of it.

I don't bring this up to tattoo Stan. It's not his fault. He doesn't count the hits. It's us actuaries up in the press box who have changed his outlook.

Stan, like a lot of others before him, suddenly woke up one day and realized there was more to this game than mere winning or losing. It's giving a new meaning to that old bromide, "It's not whether you won or lost, it's how you played the game." Put another way, "It's not whether you won or lost, but whether you got your 347th triple, your 800th base-on-balls, or your 400th lifetime home run."

I sometimes wonder why the Cardinals don't just suit up Musial and a bookkeeper. You wonder whether he's playing for the pennant or the World Almanac. When the Cardinals come to town, they are announced as "Stan Musial *and* the St. Louis Cardinals" almost as if the St. Louis Cardinals were just a trained seal act they brought along to fill the dull spots.

It's getting completely out of hand. A home run is nothing nowadays if you don't have to measure it. Pretty soon, anything under 400 feet will only count as a sacrifice fly.

The loudspeaker crackles with excitement when the home team is behind 14–0 in the eighth inning and the local Hall-of-Fame candidate gets a hit. "Ladies and Gentlemen, that was old Hardhead Harrison's 2000th lifetime hit, putting him in eleventh place in the lifetime hit standing." Since it looked just like the other 1999 hits Hardhead rapped, I don't expect anyone really came to the park just to see Hardhead hit it. But it creates a real flap in the press box.

I have felt for a long time that there were players who succumbed totally to this insidious figure fallacy. The annals of baseball are barnacled with the names of players who led their teams to pennants in their youth but turned to protecting only their own precious image as the years rolled on. Ty Cobb hung up nearly every record in the book. But where were the pennants? In the first three or four years. After that, Ty Cobb became bigger than a mere pennant.

Actually, averages are meaningless. A pitcher with a great outfield may have an earned-run-average out of all proportion to his curve ball. A pitcher with a small ball park may win a pennant for his team and still allow five runs a game. The team that sets the double-play record is usually in the second-division and thus gets enough traffic on the base paths to do it. Chuck Klein seemed one of the great hitters of baseball when he was with the old Philadelphia Phillies and had a 250-foot fence and mediocre pitching to look at. When he got traded to a contender, the Cubs, he got a steady diet of front-line pitching and dropped sixty-seven points in a year.

I felt like throwing my hat in the air and cheering the other day when Walt Alston told a reporter that if he were managing the Yankees and Mantle and Maris came down to the last day of the season needing one homer to break Ruth's record and the Yankees needed one game to win the pennant, he wouldn't hesitate to bunt either or both of them.

And he said if he were on the other team, he wouldn't hesitate to walk either or both of them.

Walt's point was that baseball is a team game, not an exercise in addition. I applaud. I don't see anything laudatory about a player who knows down to the last at-bat what his own average is but isn't sure which division his team is in.

There are some guys with so many records they need help just to carry them around with them. Their life story looks like an adding machine with a stutter.

I don't see why they don't go all the way with their biography and in addition to lifetime hits, runs, and homers, put the whole thing in stats. "Old Hardhead's lifetime bus rides totalled 12,000. He ate 15,000 eggs, 11,241 of them fried and the rest scrambled. He drank 24,001 beers, got in 1272 fights, 610 with his own team mates and the rest with spectators. He bought seventeen watches lifetime and stole three others and leads all other active players in both categories."

I mean, why not?

The Grand Old Game

By and large, baseball writers and baseball managers get along like husband and wife. They respect each other, but not much.

I bug Walt Alston something terrible, for instance, because he thinks I don't know anything about the game of baseball. Angel Manager Bill Rigney, on the other hand, is different. He *knows* I don't know anything about the game of baseball. Where Alston gets mad and stomps out when I try to be helpful, Rig waits for his laugh. He digs his elbow in my ribs and says "What do we do now, Maestro —punt?"

This breaks everybody up, but I resent it. Because I do, too, know something about baseball. Oh, not the la-de-da, fancy-schmancy game these guys play. It's the *real* game I know.

I was talking to my friend, the author, Jack Olsen, about it just the other night at the game. There in front of us on a manicured field, worked over by three shifts of grounds-keepers, guarded by a hundred ushers, policed by four umpires and with a fresh ball every other batter, they were playing a masquerade known as baseball. What a humbug!

Olsen started it all. "What," he mused, "ever became of the 'drop'?"

That made me very sad. "Yeah," I answered. "And the 'inshoot' and the 'outshoot' and the 'hook.' They don't make pitches like they used to any more." Jack was gloomy, too. "Know what they call a 'slow ball' nowadays?" he demanded. "A 'change-up'! Now, I ask you!"

The game has gone to hell, I say. Why, these guys don't have the slightest idea what the game of baseball really is. How can a pitcher get the real flavor of the game when they yank him out of there just because he gives up six hits in one inning! Why, I used to give up six hits before I got a guy out. We *never* changed pitchers when I played the game. That was because the pitcher was the guy who owned the ball.

Jack in his book *Over the Fence Is Out* told of the time his catcher came out to complain "I think you're losing your stuff." This, just because they got twelve runs off him that inning. "Whose ball we using?" Jack challenged him. "Yours," admitted the catcher. "Then I ain't losing my stuff," Jack growled. Not till they lost the ball, anyway.

That was the way we played it. If we lost the ball, we carried on with a tennis ball. You could make that do things a moth couldn't do. But the batters took a toe-hold because it couldn't hurt them.

We never got sore arms. And this was remarkable because if the ball didn't get lost, merely got the cover knocked off, we just wrapped it in enough tape to make a mummy. You couldn't really throw that ball. You had to shot-put it. Of course, our pitcher wasn't 60 feet 6 inches from home plate. The lots weren't that big. And the catcher didn't squat right under the batter with an iron mask and a mattress with straps and shin armor on. Our catcher stood 10 feet back where he caught the ball on one bounce, sometimes right in the eyeglasses. Of course, if the batter fouled one off, he caught that in his teeth.

What do these guys know of pressure? Did they ever have to pitch and watch their kid sister at the same time? Pressure is when you get two out and the bases loaded and some kid comes running down the street and says "Say, is that your kid sister hanging off a cliff down there?" That's when you know you got to get the guy out in a hurry because if she falls you'll catch the dickens at home.

I think anybody that plays the outfield in grass that's been cut is a sissy. Where we played, you wouldn't have been able to see the top of Albie Pearson's head. The infield wasn't much better. We had a rock for first base and you couldn't see it, you could feel it. You didn't need an umpire because you could always tell when a guy reached first. That's because he tripped and yelled "ouch!"

You never lost your star players because of injuries. But their mothers sure had a lot to say about the pennant race. We lost more games because a window would fly open some place and a mother's voice would float over saying "John, you get right home here and make your bed!" I'd like to see Willie Davis play his best and be half-listening for the sound of his mother's voice at the same time.

We didn't have umpires. It was more fun to fight. Your

right fielder was always a guy who didn't play baseball too good but who could fight like Jimmy McLarnin who was the neighborhood idol. You won a lot of games with your fists.

You also won them with your fingers. We used to choose up sides by palming our hands on a bat and the guy whose fist last closed around it got "first ups." This was important because sometimes there weren't any "second-ups" or "last-ups." With us, it was a legal game anyway.

Rig and Alston got their nerve. I know more about this cotton-picking game than these guys with trappers' mitts and tricked-up bats and brand-new balls and canvas bases and sun glasses. They don't have to worry about breaking windows. They don't have to hide the No TRESPASSING. THIS MEANS YOU! signs. They don't use a spoke wheel from an old Essex for home plate.

They don't know nothin' about the game of baseball.

The Big Spenders

My notion is, I'd like to get in a no-limit poker game with the owners of major league baseball. Either that or have the gold-brick concession on the streets where they live. I mean, these guys have got to be the all-time soft touches.

Compared to them, a guy who bets into a pat full house with a pair of eights and a kicker is a piker. I swear, if any other class of human beings popped the bankroll for the high-priced but shoddy merchandise these fellows go for, they'd be screaming to the Better Business Bureau.

Yet, here they go again, like housewives at a bargain basement, panting and hollering, elbowing each other out of the way, waving fistfuls of greenbacks in the air and doubling and redoubling the bid with each hoarse shout —laying a cool $10,000,000 on the line for a lot of sky pie, rainbow gold, watered stocks, and brass rings. You know what I mean. The Bonus Kids.

The thing is, don't these guys *ever* learn?

How many Bonus Kids can you name right off hand who are still in the big leagues? Dave Nicholson? Uh-uh. He'll have to pay to see Baltimore play this year. Not that he can't afford it. On the money Baltimore paid him a few years ago he can pay his way into home games (box seats) until the year 2461 and still have enough left over to tip the usher.

Baltimore, which was going the other way on the field, used to lead the league in bonus spending in the mid-1950s and once they dealt off $36,000 to a fast ball pitcher named Bruce Swango. Bruce was a terror in the cornfields. But he had one slight flaw. Crowds terrified him.

Now, this would not have been a problem with the old St. Louis Browns but at Baltimore there was occasionally a quorum present. When there was, Bruce was so self-conscious he couldn't find home plate through his blushes. He didn't give the money back, all the same.

Probably the most famous Bonus Boy was Paul Pettit. In 1949, Lefty Paul was the most sought-after high school player in the nation. A flashy pitcher with Narbonne High, the son of an English-born milkman, Paul had struck out 390 batters in three years, twenty-seven of them in one (extra-inning) game. He had pitched three no-hitters in a row, and the scouts assured their front offices that his fast ball didn't hop—it high-jumped.

Paul had ivory hunters from six big league clubs camped in his living room when he graduated. Their jaws dropped when they found out what they were up against: a Hollywood agent had beaten them to the boy. One Fred Stephani had signed him for $85,000. At first baseball was in a snit and threatened to have nothing to do with a boy who had gone Hollywood. Then they remembered the fast ball, swallowed their pride, bought out Stephani and signed Pettit for $100,000.

Stephani retained the motion picture and TV rights to Pettit's career. Presumably, he still has them. So far as baseball is concerned, he can have Pettit too. In the third week of his career, Paul hung a curve ball in New Orleans against a batter named Norm Zauchin, popped an elbow and was through.

When last seen, Paul was wearing glasses and trying to re-establish a career as a first baseman and outfielder in the deep bushes. He couldn't even throw batting practice.

Minor league outfields are full of Paul Pettits and Dave Nicholsons. A lot of other Bonus Babies went back to hang around street corners like any other normal American boy. Only difference was, organized baseball was paying them about $10,000 a year to do it.

"What," I asked the Dodgers' Fresco Thompson, "is the wisdom of all this?"

"There isn't any," Fresco said candidly. "In 1922, I was all-city shortstop in New York City and I never even saw a scout. I wrote to an owner in Grand Island, Nebraska, and he said if I could get out there, he'd give me a look-see. I took a bus, on my own money, made good, and got a whole $75 a month.

"Today, all baseball knows that the hungry player is a good player. So when they get a good boy they make sure right away he'll never be hungry. The first thing he does is get a bright red convertible and an apartment that looks like a cartoon in *Playboy*. Then some hungry kid beats him out of a job and then realizes it's going to take him ten years to get as much money as Golden Boy already got. So he gets sore and sulks. Wisdom? You tell me."

This Is Baseball?

All right, class, our subject for today will be "So You Think You Know Baseball?" We'll begin the general questioning with the front row and move right on back. Ready? Places, everybody, please.

Now, remember, one answer and one answer only. If you're not sure, just leave it blank. All set? Here goes:

Q. Now, the ballpark is antiquated, rotting in the beams and coming apart in the joints. What is it?

A. Steeped in tradition.

Q. Splendid! Now, the manager of the home team is what?

A. Astute. Canny. A grizzled master of the game.

Q. Even if he's illiterate?

A. Especially if he's illiterate.

Q. Capital! Class, you really have a grasp of our subject. Now, what do we call a schizophrenic who climbs the backstops, spits at the fans, swings on his teammates and lies down on home plate?

A. He's a holler guy. He's good for the game.

Q. Excellent! And precisely correct. Now, what is a man who hits an annual forty home runs, bats .320 and averages 140 runs-batted-in but keeps his mouth shut, goes home every night and minds his own business?

A. He's not a take-charge guy. He can't lead.

Q. Right! And who is a leader, a take-charge guy?

A. A shortstop who can't hit .250, is slow in the field and a lousy baserunner but who never keeps his mouth closed, answers to the nickname "Yappy," fights with umpires and calls .300 hitters "bushers."

Q. Now, you've got it! And what do we say about a character like that who can't hit, run or field but can holler?

A. He comes to play. He's our pennant insurance.

Q. Exactly. And he's the most popular guy in the league. With whom?

A. The other managers. He's *their* pennant insurance, too. He's the surest out in the league and they sit up nights praying he doesn't get laryngitis and get waived out of the majors.

Q. I don't know when I've tested a sharper batch of students. Now, tell me, what do we say about the pitcher who can't get his curve to break so he takes it out on the hitters by throwing at their heads?

A. He beats himself. He'd win twenty games if he could control himself.

Q. And would he?

A. Not if he joined a monastery. He loses his temper because he loses his fast ball, not vice versa. When he's going good, his wife can't get him in a fight.

Q. Marvelous! Now, nicknames. The player's name is Robert and he's a pitcher. In ten seconds, what is he known as?

A. Rapid Robert. Bullet Bob.

Q. Right! But supposing he's got a fast ball a balloon could beat to the plate?

A. It doesn't matter. His name is Robert, it's Rapid Robert. If it's Leonard, his name is "Dutch." Even if he's Irish. That's the way baseball is.

Q. Good, good! Now, what do we call the has-been who can't get around on a fast ball any more, has slowed up in the field but beats the whole squad to a bar stool and has the best "book" on the girls in every town they hit?

A. The old pro.

Q. And what do we mean by a pitcher who is a "stopper"?

A. A guy who will beat the Phillies for you just after you have lost four straight and the league lead to the Braves.

Q. And when a manager says his players are grown men and have to be treated as such, what does he mean?

A. They give the slip to his private detectives.

Q. Absolutely correct! Now, when the Sporting News hints a "sensational trade," to what does it refer?

A. Two disappointing teams get together to swap failures.

Q. Right. And what is meant by a general manager who is a "regular David Harum"?

A. He swaps a .260 hitter for a .270 hitter.

Q. Excellent! And who was the greatest trader in the history of baseball?

A. Walter O'Malley. He traded the Brooklyn Dodgers for downtown L.A.

Q. Is baseball a business?

A. If it isn't, General Motors is a sport.

Next Voice You Hear

My friend, Phil Huber, the demon realtor from Riverside, is a man who is fed up. The pap he gets on the pregame and post-game interview shows smacks to him of dishonest journalism. He yearns to hear these institutions of baseball as they really *should* sound.

For instance—

The manager of the fourteenth place club is being interviewed in the clubhouse before the game.

Q. Now, Skip, I notice our club is having a little difficulty getting started—lost fifteen out of our last fourteen if you include that forfeit game where the boys got lost on the way to the ball park and failed to show up. Tell me, do you think things will look up?

A. Are you kidding? Lissen. You saw that infield. Tell me, was Charlie Chaplin ever funnier?

Q. Heh-heh. Well, Skip, now that's a question. But what about old Harry Hardthrow, the mainstay of our mound staff? How's the old arm coming along?

A. Arm? What are you talking about? It was his jaw his wife broke. Harry never even saw the frying pan coming. In fact, that blonde he was with was lucky it didn't hit her, too.

Q. Ah, well, heh-heh. Every team has its little problems. What about old Jackie Shorthop, the third-baseman? Do you think shifting him to the outfield will help?

A. If I had my way I'd shift him to the Spokane outfield but I understand the manager there would quit if we did. I won't say he's clumsy. But I got him a spot on a Gillette commercial demonstrating a razor and he cut himself shaving.

Q. What about the youngsters, Skip? They're coming along, aren't they?

A. Well, if you mean they ain't harmed themselves seriously. As far as baseball is concerned those guys couldn't make the ground crew.

Q. Old Barney Bullwhip has come up with a case of the virus, I see.

A. Virus? The only virus he's got, you get in a bottle. He's got a hangover is what he's got. If he wasn't the only guy I got can throw the ball straight over to first base, I'd turn him over to Alcoholics Anonymous. I got only one thing going for me with Barney. He's been thrown out of 70 percent of the bars in this town. When he gets thrown out of the other 30 percent he might start showing up in shape to pitch.

Then, there is the post-game interview. Same cast of characters.

Q. Well, Skipper, do you think your boys looked any better losing tonight than they did losing the last 14?

A. Well, I'll say one thing for the guys: they didn't quit. Not even when they were down twenty-four runs. On the other hand, I've heard of coming from behind—but twenty-four *runs!?* We had a close one last week—14–3.

Q. But the boys weren't downhearted?

A. Downhearted? Not this bunch! They eat like they were on a winning streak. They lead the league in steaks. Also in passed balls, errors, strikeouts and having three men on the same base at the same time. These guys *back* into the record books. We'll be leading in suicides if we keep losing.

Q. But there's nothing wrong a few base hits won't cure, eh, Skip?

A. Lissen, not even base hits can help us anymore. I mean, this team isn't in the cellar, it's in a *mine*. Two more losses and we're liable to run into Floyd Collins. The fans'll get the bends just coming to the game.

Q. Skip, this is not to criticize but a few of us were wondering why you didn't put old Bagman Barnes in there in the late innings.

A. Couldn't find him. He was out in the clubhouse on the phone to his bookie.

Q. Heh-heh. Boys will be boys. Betting the races, eh?

A. Well, I *hope* it was the races. That's what we told the FBI.

Q. Well, Skip, thank you for another informative interview on our own Canvasbacks, the pride of our city. And on behalf of our sponsors I would like to present you with our product, this genuine Ivy League, belt-in-the-back, nylon-reinforced strait jacket. And remember, if you're mental—call rental.

Follies of Baseball

The other night, at the Coliseum, the Dodgers and the Phillies put on a special series of contests before the game —egg-throwing, wheelbarrow-racing, and the like. They do this at Phillies games so someone will show up besides the Phillies.

Now, this is all right with me as far as it goes. But I would have in mind something more authentically baseball, something that goes hand-in-hand with the everyday business of being a ballplayer.

For instance, Event No. 1 in my pre-game rodeo would be switch-hitting Scotch drinking, open to everybody who has not been picked up by the cops for outstanding performance in this event within the past three months. Such contestants will be deemed to have lost their amateur standing and ineligible to take on rookies, if any.

Event No. 2 will be freestyle money-counting and will be restricted to Bonus Babies with no bills under $20 denomination entered. Winner will be the one who can count his bonus before the end of the game.

No. 3 event will be Girl-Chasing with ten points for waitresses, twelve points for college girls, and fifty points for girls who don't particularly like baseball. Winner gets a free phone call home to the wife.

There will be a special contest for pinchhitters to see which can make himself the most invisible in the dugout when the manager wants him to go up and hit against Drysdale just after someone has cracked a home run off him.

For relief pitchers, there will be competition to see who can fake a back injury most convincingly when asked to go in and get Henry Aaron or Willie Mays out. First prize will be a screen test.

Event No. 7 will be water-cooler-kicking for managers only.

Coaches will be tested for ability to wave runners in with no chance. First place will go to the coach whose man is out by 89 feet or less.

Handle-hitting for .200 hitters should see the largest entry of the list of the night, there are so many of them in the league. First prize will be a banjo.

Brush-back pitching against live targets will be a popular event—with everybody but the targets. Don Drysdale will have to take a handicap of two knock-downs if he is entered, three if the batter is Frank Robinson. Winner gets a lifesize statue of Frank Robinson to practice on in his room.

There will be the Band-Aid award to the runner who comes in with spikes highest in the slide. For the infielder, consolation prize will be a year's supply of sutures—or four free transfusions, whichever he needs most urgently at the moment.

The Eichmann award will go to the second-baseman who can break the most base-runners' teeth with the tag. Booby prize for runners will be a credit card to a credit dentist.

The speed events will include a contest to see who can get out of the back door of a saloon fastest when he sees the Old Man coming in the front.

Tip-toeing past the manager's hotel room at 3 o'clock in the morning will be restricted to managers who are light sleepers and players who are heavy drinkers. Losing managers will get a hearing-aid; losing players, crepe-soled shoes.

Prizes for faking a shaving commercial when you've already shaved that day will be an electric razor or a false mustache.

A contest for swinging at curve balls that bounce will be refereed by Dick Stuart, the all-time champion at the event.

There will be an exhibition of bat-rolling (with spikes on) by Larry Sherry and soap-sliding (barefoot) by Drysdale against the clock with points awarded for three-point falls. A multiple fracture will retire the trophy permanently. Also the player.

The evening will conclude with a shin-kicking contest with Leo Durocher taking on all four umpires. Crutches will be supplied by Sales Boosters Inc., whoever they are, and the event will be sponsored by Mercurochrome.

There will be three door prizes—one for the ballplayer who has run up the biggest tab at the House of Serfas, one for the fan who makes it back to the saloon bus in a straight line, and one for the sportswriter who gets out of the losing pitcher's locker room without his glasses broken after he asks what kind of a pitch the home run that won the game was hit off.

The singer who sings "The Star-Spangled Banner" *on* key will be sent back to Spokane for more seasoning.

Forever, Cuddles

VERO BEACH—Letter from a rookie's wife:

Dearest Darling:

How are you? I am fine and think of you every day, never mind what your mother says.

I am working now at the Bon Ton Grill, which is really fixed up since they got the liquor in. All the fellows from the box works ask for you and say, "Boy. I bet if that old husband of yours could only see you in them net stockings he'd bat a thousand." Even that goofy Neddie Sparks, who you never liked, had to say something nice. He said I must of sent you a picture because you hit one all the way to the pitcher yesterday.

Darling, I have great news for you. I've taken in a roomer. You remember that guy you said looked like a fellow in the movies who was forever kissing a girl's hand and asking her to Tango? Well, he told me he like to went nuts over at the Widow Abernethy's because there wasn't anybody over there who liked to dance. He moved in yesterday and he's teaching me the Bossa Nova. I let him have your old house slippers and he's driving the car just till he gets his fixed.

The other night was election night and the bar had to be closed; so I had the whole gang over to our house. Somebody broke that silly old statue they gave you in the International League last season.

Someone else burned a hole in the rug, but they put the fire out right away.

The party wasn't as noisy as the papers said. A few of the guys were doing the Cha-Cha-Cha and when Tub Turner threw that glass, why it broke the big picture window. But still I didn't see why the police came. Not even when Dick and Jack took to fighting on the front lawn.

A Mr. O'Malley called and said it was important, but that was about the time the police came and, what with the sirens and trying to keep them from throwing Dick and Jack in the police wagon and all, I didn't catch all of it. He said, "What's going on over there; it sounds like a raid," and I said, "Oh, Mr. O'Malley, my husband said you were a great kidder and I said I sure was glad my husband had a great sense of humor and Mr. O'Malley said, "I bet you are," and hung up.

It got real hot at the party so we all went swimming in the pool which I forgot to tell you I had put in. Mr. Hodges said that now you were in the big leagues your credit was good as gold and signing over the house was just a formality.

It's really terrif, the pool, which you'll enjoy as soon as the season's over if it doesn't get too cool by then. I put on my Bikini and all the guys followed me out to the pool.

Such nuts. When I went in, lots of them jumped in with their clothes on. I must say your mother got a distorted version of *that*.

Spec McGee, the sport writer, was over and he said you have a new nickname, "Double Play" Dugan, and Harry, my boss, said, "That's funny, I didn't know Dugie was an infielder" and Spec said, "He isn't."

Darling, what do you play anyway? Are you a halfback or something? I want to learn all about baseball because your life is my life now and I read every issue of the sport page and was real proud of myself when I read to Cesar (that's our roomer, Darling, and that's not his real name, but I call him that because he looks so much like Cesar Romero —only much younger, of course). I said, "Cesar, my husband is batting .350." And Cesar says, "That's not his batting average; that's his fielding average" and I was even prouder of you. I think it's thrilling and I told Cesar so just the other night when we were having dinner by candlelight. "You're right," he told me. "Your husband is the only guy I know of who throws a change-of-pace from the outfield." He's one of your biggest fans.

I gave him those old golf sticks of yours because he said he had left his on his estate in Spain because they were heirlooms and had been in his family since the days of Queen Isabella. I wanted to hear more, but his friend, Gabby, choked just as he said it and his face turned red and tears came to his eyes. He had a napkin in his throat and Cesar says, "It's one of those attacks he gets. He's a hemophiliac which is a rare disease of the laugh glands and the only thing he can do is laugh uproariously till it goes away." And, thank Heaven, Gabby took the napkin out of his mouth and laughed and laughed till he was all right.

Darling, thanks for the money. I lent part of it to Harry,

the part that was left over after we fixed the car. Oh, I forgot to tell you, my brother had an accident with the car. I think the woman will live. It's a good thing, too, because I told them I was driving on account of Buddy's license was revoked last year—the time he ran into the river with that Waters girl. You remember, the judge told him his license was revoked till the girl got out of the wheel chair. Well, I think Buddy got a raw deal because that looks like that'll be never.

Harry will be writing you a letter to see if you can talk some sense into his wife. It's about that night Harry took me home after work and he said, "Let's drive up along the river bank, I want to discuss business with you." We hadn't been up there more than two hours when his wife jerks open the door and says, "Oh, no, you don't. Not this hussy, too." And I says, "I beg your pardon, I happen to be Mrs. Dugan" and Harry's wife says, "You're just a number, Dearie. No. 14." She's awfully jealous of Harry. Spec says he can't for the life of him understand why. Spec has a funny way of saying things and Gabby had another attack when he said that and he said he had to laugh till his sides hurt or it'd take hold of him.

Darling, if you think of it, will you pay the I. Magnin's bill? They threatened to take back the mink coat if I didn't. I told you about the mink coat, didn't I? The one I bought to go up to Las Vegas over the weekend? Anyway, it's beautiful. Cesar borrowed it for the weekend to show his mother.

I got a kind of a sore head today. It might be all the champagne I drank but my ankle is all swollen up, too. They said I hurt it when I was doing the Twist on top of the piano, but I can't remember a thing from last night.

I told Harry I thought they were pulling my leg and Harry said they sure were.

Well, Darling, please make a lot of field goals or pop-ups (Spec said you lead the league in them already and the only guy who can catch you is the team fungo hitter), and I'm so proud of you and hurry home to your little baby who, I told Spec, will be keeping a lookout in the window for you (Spec said I'd be better to keep it out on the lawn). I sure want you to meet Cesar, too, and he wants to meet you and feels terrible he had to take this long business trip just the time you come home.

But you'll meet him. He'll come back. He has to; he has the car.

Faithfully yours, Cuddles.

P.S.: That's what the boys call me. Don't you think it's cute?

Dignified Interview

(*FT. LAUDERDALE, Fla.—Baseball slugger Roger Maris, major league home-run champion, announced Tuesday that henceforth he will give no more interviews to the press on the subject of baseball. Unhappy over recent stories, the slugger announced: "I'll be friendly. I'll talk to the writers about other things but no more interviews on baseball."—News Item.*)

If Roger Maris is as good as his word, stand by for the biggest revolution in the history of sports journalism.

All the idea has to do is catch on with other players, and the art of the baseball interview may never be the same and the reading matter may drive Hedda Hopper into the Baseball Writers of America, Beverly Hills chapter. *The Sporting News* will have to hire Dorothy Kilgallen—or Jack Paar.

Imagine, if you will, the following fictitious interview between that celebrated first baseman of the New York Donkeys, "Swats" Murphy, the greatest swinger in the game, and the golden-tongued oracle of the sportscasters, Buddy Blabber. They are just about to go on the air.

Swats (fastening mike around his neck): "Now, remember, Blabber. Nothing about baseball. Right?"

Buddy Blabber: "Right, Swatter. OK, we're on the air . . . Good afternoon, sports fans. This is Buddy Blabber bringing you an exclusive interview with the greatest fielding first baseman in Donkey history, Swats Murphy. Swats, first of all, how's the wife?"

Swats: "She's still running around with that bartender, Bud, but as soon as she stops giving the shake to my private detectives, I'll catch up to her. Actually, I could divorce her right now. On the grounds she keeps hiding my teeth so I can't go out."

Buddy: "I see. Fine, fine, Swats. And the kids, how are they?"

Swats: "The oldest boy is just fine, Bud. Should be out on parole any day now. We've got his old room ready. Of course, we've hidden the counterfeiting machine for the present."

Buddy: "And the baby, Swats?"

Swats: "Well, we got him to stop smoking. Once we get him to stop pulling the wings out of canaries and letting the air out of police motorcycles, we feel he'll be OK. The post office made him stop that mail-order business. Said they didn't understand where a kid like him got pictures like that in the first place."

Buddy: "Swats, how's the training going . . ."

Swats (wagging a warning finger): "Uh-uh-uh. None of that, now."

Buddy (hastily): "Oh, I meant *after* hours, Swats."

Swats: "Well, I got kicked out of the Kit-Kat Club last night. Just because I tripped the whole chorus line."

Buddy: "They objected, eh?"

Swats: "Never saw a bunch with a lousier sense of humor in my life, particularly the one that's suing. I'll say this: if she got a busted back, then I'm Yogi Berra."

Buddy: "But the new white Cadillac is breaking in nicely, eh, Swats?"

Swats: "Yeah, as soon as we get the blood off the fender."

Buddy: "Blood?!"

Swats: "Yeah, where I hit that kid over in Tampa. You know. They called it hit-and-run but I just couldn't get the engine to stop running. For eight miles."

Buddy: "How's the kid?"

Swats: "Oh, fine. He's really getting the hang of the wheel-chair. He'll be OK when he figures out reverse on that thing. He'll be set for the next ten years."

Buddy: "Well, you look in great shape, Swats."

Swats: "I'm getting there, Buddy. I've cut out the martinis before breakfast and I figure by the time I taper off to three before lunch, I'll be ready. The waistline is trimming down fine. I saw the edge of my shoelaces and toes this morning without bending forward."

Buddy (desperately): "Swats, just this one *personal* question. Do you think if you just roll your wrists a little bit on the hitting surface of the bat . . ."

Swats (red-faced, red-necked, bawling out): "*Casey*, get

a cop to throw this bum out, he's starting to ask *personal* questions about my batting!"

Saga of Ol' Case

The spiked shoes have a high polish on them but the legs growing out of them look like nothing seen on a human form since man wore leopard skin. They weren't born, they were whittled. They have so many lumps in them, they look like two sacks of peanuts. They are directionless, and so bowed and bent they look as if he is preparing to jump even when he's standing erect.

The face is the color of flour and water. When he twists it, it's so mobile it looks like the world's biggest wad of bubble gum. The mammoth nose is hooked but the eyes are a bright and merry blue and as inquisitive as a child's.

You look at Casey Stengel and you have to resist the temptation to ask him what ever became of Snow White. He doesn't belong to the real world. He belongs in the pages of Grimms' Fairy Tales. Or peering out of a tree in the Black Forest.

He's the only man in the world who has his own language, two banks, a golf course, a blue serge suit, and non-stop speech. There are so many books about him on the newsstand, you'd think he'd just discovered a cure for Elizabeth Taylor.

He didn't start life as a baseball player. He wanted to be a dentist. A left-handed dentist. But he found his first tooth extraction tougher to solve than a low curve ball and bloodier than a Fourth of July weekend. As he recounts it in his autobiography, the patient had tears in his eyes and blood on his shirt as Casey struggled with a tooth that wanted to stay where it was. "I made the mistake of not putting the chair low enough," he alibis ruefully. "Finally, the instructor said, 'Would it do you some good to lower the chair?' After that, the only people that would take a chance with me practicing dentistry were my parents."

The most successful manager in the history of the American League, Casey has never got out of the second division in the National. And this year he only hopes to be able to stay in it. When last seen, his Mets appeared to be chopping a hole in the bottom of the league and getting ready to bail out of baseball. They lost seven straight games in their sweep West and the word out of San Francisco was that anyone who saw the team heading for the Golden Gate Bridge was to call the cops.

The team even got so unnerved its pitchers began throwing at Willie Mays which is the next step to a crackup because Mays is tough enough to get out even when he's not mad.

I caught up with Casey and his athletes on their way through Chavez Ravine where Casey almost had to spend the night when he was late in showering and got to the exit just as the last park policeman was barricading it. "He tells me 'Seventeen other cops have gone home, why not me?'" Casey explained. "So I sez, 'What about me, do I have to go back now with the lights shut off and no water in the place and here I have my relations waiting and it's my home town over there?' So the next night, I went home two ways and then yesterday I went to three places in Glendale which was one of my banks and my next trip I'll get to the next bank, and that was my best pitcher they beat and did you see where he pitched that ball to that big fella

(Howard) who you can fool at the plate pretty good only not when you don't throw the sinker?"

Someone cleared his throat. "How," he asked, "do you like it back in the National League, Case?"

"Ma-a-ahvelous! Outstanding!" Casey greeted him. "Now I have some amazin' players—outstanding players which will shock you and we have this here Hickey (Ed. note: Centerfielder Jim Hickman) which I am going to keep whether anybody likes it or not even though he takes too many pitches.

"This is a team which will shock you and amaze you but not all the time and I am not running for office but I'm making a study of the players for two years to see if we can give you some competition, y'unnerstand. Now I'm back in this here game because of all these outstanding new stadiums which are going to be so beautiful like this here one only you will notice that the outfield is too large for the ability of some of my players and they keep this infield hard because somebody tells me you can't catch this team that plays here as they are all too fast to be seen with the naked eye—

"But now you look over at that other league and there is this Pepperoni (Ed. note: Joe Pepitone) nobody knew who he was till the day before yesterday or how to pronounce his name and I got some men who are unknown too, but I was saving my pitcher until I got ahead in the seventh inning, but I never got ahead and I said to my other pitcher that I better take him out, people were beginning to talk. Now there's three things you can do: you can win or you can lose. Or it can rain. And it said it would rain here but I musta been reading some foreign papers as they tell me it never rains here in the summer."

There was a stunned silence. "You mean," someone took a longshot, "your team will improve?"

"That's what I just said," said Casey.

Two's a Crowd

The trouble with the Mantle-Maris story is that it comes in duplicate—a complication man has been hard put to cope with since the Garden of Eden.

Americans like their heroes solo—like "The Lone Eagle," "The Lone Ranger," "The Manassa Mauler," "The Brown Bomber," "The Bambino," "The Terre Haute Terror," "Tarzan of the Apes," "Jack Armstrong," and "Little Orphan Annie." The Bobbsey Twins, after all, never quite cut it.

Now along come Mantle and Maris, tandem heroes on a bicycle built for one, and an essential element is lost. The worship is diluted, or, worse yet, confused. The god has two heads. The situation is intolerable. "Togetherness" has no place in the mythology of sports. My guy is an immortal. Yours is a bum, period. The way it should be.

What happens then when two guys are trying to get on the same pedestal is that one of them becomes the heavy. The other one becomes Our Nell.

This is how history has overtaken Roger Maris.

Maris in the spring was a liked and likable young man whose mission in life was to be to take his place alongside, but slightly below, Mickey Mantle. He could hit thirty or forty home runs, mind his manners, play right field, and take his place on the bubble-gum cards with the rest of the sub-immortals. Under no circumstances was he expected to disturb the repose of Babe Ruth, of all things.

Now, Maris in the fall is a young guy who has missed the whole point. He is the St. Bernard who drinks the brandy himself. He is baseball's answer to John Wilkes Booth. At the Hall of Fame, you hear the ghostly whispers, "Who asked *him?*"

The first, startling result of this piece of upstart-ery is the sudden deification of Mantle. Before Maris, Mickey was always just the guy who had the nerve to try to take the place of the great Joe DiMaggio. He got booed more than a cop taking a ball away from a kid with crutches. Something close to hate showered down on him each time he took his place in the batter's box.

But since the siege of Maris, an astonishing and violent reaction has set in at Yankee Stadium, if not in baseball. The rabble has discovered it loved Mantle all the time. What showers down on him now for the first time in his career is unallayed idolatry. "I wouldn't have believed it," New York writer Stan Isaacs told me, "but you could almost feel the waves of love coming down over Mickey the last game at the stadium. The people who used to throw brickbats were throwing kisses."

The turnabout would mystify no psychologist of sport. The fan who boos frequently does so out of an excess of love. He is insulating himself against the probability of his hero letting him down. He is the little kid who says, "I don't want to go anyway," just in case he doesn't get asked. He is the cynic who cares so deeply he conceals it with a sneer.

Whatever Maris does to Babe Ruth, this is what he has done for Mantle. He has made it possible for his fans to love without shame.

The relationship of Mantle and Maris is without parallel in the pages of sport. Forced by fate into the most frenzied kind of career competition, they are more than friends. They room together in an apartment in Queens where they guard their privacy as zealously as a Russian spy. They appear to need each other as much as the Yankees need them.

They share not adjoining lockers but back-to-back lockers so they can better accommodate the crush of press who crowd around after a game like flies around a side of fresh meat.

They are as dissimilar as Anna and the King of Siam. Mantle is a dead-pan, uncommunicative. Roger is lively, quotable. Mickey never starts a conversation. Maris never stops one. Mickey is forbearing to the point of sainthood. Or appears to be. The youngsters Jimmy Piersall slugged and booted out of centerfield Mantle wouldn't have turned around to look at. Maris is what baseball calls a "red-neck"—or, at least, that part of the anatomy will do for the moment.

Maris protests he doesn't care about the home run record. Mickey really doesn't. Mantle is a good listener. If Maris is listening it is to the sound of his own voice. The only time they huddle together is when their agent, Frank Scott, enters the dressing room, sewing up contracts for everything from candy pellets to the Perry Como Show. He talks volubly of a half-a-million dollars. That 61st home run should land fittingly in a Brink's truck. Mantle only listens. Maris asks questions.

Maris criticizes umpires on page one in the papers. Mantle criticizes them under his breath as he walks away from the plate. Mantle scans the golf scores, the football scores.

He would rather talk about either than baseball. Maris talks about Maris.

After ten years as the biggest name in the biggest city on earth, Mantle is a country boy. He is held up as a kind of Mortimer Snerd with a home run swing but he is not without mirth, not without flashes of insight that show he observes more than he lets on. But after years of appearing in public before 2,000,000 people a year, he still distrusts strangers.

Mickey talks to individuals, never to groups. Maris talks to people as though he were addressing the U.S. Senate. Neither can ever hope to achieve the Jovian dimensions of Ruth. Mantle wouldn't want to, wouldn't give enough of himself. Maris wouldn't be able to but may leave the stamp of his personality more readably in the pages of time.

Mantle will remain an enigma. No man says with authority, "I understand Mickey Mantle." Mantle is in a cocoon of his own choosing. Mantle finds baseball easy, the rest of life difficult. Maris is more at home away than on the field. Mantle powers a baseball out of a park by brute strength. Maris flicks them on a line at a dead pull. Maris' homers land in the sixth row. Mantle's land downtown.

The suspicion that Mickey is more deserving of the mantle has crept over baseball. Maris has not batted over .300 for a full season since he left the deep minors seven years ago. Mantle can bat .300 at will. Maris had never hit more than forty home runs before. Mantle hit more than forty three times, and more than fifty once.

More than just years have passed since anyone hit sixty home runs. When Ruth hit his, we were keeping cool with Coolidge; you could tune in your crystal set and hear, "Don't Bring Lulu." If you were hep you said, "You tell 'em, kid, 'cause I-I stutter." College kids wore raccoon coats with a flask in them and the rumble seat was the cat's pajamas or the bee's knees. Helen Twelvetrees was playing in the movie at the Bijou.

Today we're in the atomic age. God help us. But I'll tell you something. Home run no. sixty-one will still make page one in every paper in the country and a million dollars for the guy who hits it. His name should begin with an "M."

Madison Avenue Touch

It may be the weather, it may be the general level of play, slow games or even sunspots. But there is very little doubt baseball is the Sick Man of Sports these days. Even the gilt-edged Dodgers with what appears to be a clear track to the pennant have taken to wondering where everybody went.

The Angels, who have a clear track to tenth place at the moment, are even ready for desperate measures. They are encouraging people to come out and root *against* them. For the forthcoming games with Cleveland and Detroit, they will rope off a special section in the grandstand for former residents of those cities to sit and cheer for the old home town—theirs, not ours.

I tested this idea for soundness with an old friend of mine from my magazine days, Chuck Champlin. Chuck is a reporter for *Time* but this is only a sideline. He is really one of America's foremost sloganeers, a student of the hidden persuasion, the subliminal come-on and the all-out assault of the ad man. He is in charge of the campaign for more billboards on the highway and the society for the preservation of singing commercials.

Accordingly, I thought Chuck would have a suggestion or two for the Angels. He did. He dismissed the idea of special blocks of seats for ex-Clevelanders by allowing "I am not one to encourage treason in any form—too downbeat."

He quickly switched his thoughts into gray flannel, pushed his horned rimmed glasses up on his nose—and decided that what was needed was good old Madison Avenue know-how, the old hard sell, singing commercials, dancing tomato cans, gravel-voiced jingles, nerve-grating bongo drums—the old let's-run-it-up-the-flagpole-and-see-if-anyone salutes it, or put-it-on the-club-car-and-see-if-it-gets-off-at Westport approach.

Chuck coughed. "You, of all people, Jim, will remember the terrific sales job I did on the Perry Como Doll ('Wind it up and it unwinds') with those spot commercials that consisted of forty-five seconds of gentle snoring," he reminded me, adding, "The firm incidentally came through bankruptcy in great shape."

Baseball, thinks Chuck, has the stuff of which TV commercials are made. He whipped one up which he said "I modestly think will cop the gonfalon all the way."

SOUND EFFECT: Indian war dance. Battle noises, fearful shrieks.

ANNOUNCER: (Paul Harvey, if possible) See grown men snuffed out at home plate, erased at second! See them die on third! See whole teams blasted, trimmed, whitewashed, skunked, routed. See Tribesmen initiated in the sacred rites of bunting!

SOUND EFFECT: Stampeding cattle.

ANNOUNCER: SEE ENRAGED MOUNDSMEN CHARGE THE UMPIRE BEFORE YOUR VERY

EYES. CHEER LIVE-ACTION SHAVING COM-
MERCIALS IN PERSON! THRILL TO THE PULSE-
POUNDING TEMPO OF TWO BULLPENS IN
ACTION. SEE THE ANGELS GO WHERE NO
MAN HAS EVER GONE BEFORE—TENTH
PLACE! CRINGE AS INDIANS TORTURE THEM,
TIGERS DEVOUR THEM. HEAR THE NATIVE
CHANT OF 'YANKEE GO HOME,' TELL THE
TWINS TO DROP DEAD TWICE.

Interrupted Chuck: "How can anybody resist a pitch
like that—belt-high and blazing fast?" He even had a
change of pace.

SOUND EFFECT: Soft music (borrow from Forest
Lawn if possible).

ANNOUNCER: Hi, there, friends of radioland. Like
fresh air but worried about smog? Two out of three balloon
tests show there's less smog at night, two-to-one. Come out
to Wrigley Field and breathe deeply. Remember, too, the
air is changed regularly by a stiff breeze from fashionable
Redondo Beach imported at no cost to you by the management.

The parking problem slows Chuck down not one bit.
"You and I know, Jim," he says, "that with the kind of
crowds we've been having the only people with parking
problems are parking lot owners. I think it's just as well not
to broadcast volleyball games from the parking lots between
innings—bruise the image—but I think I have the solu-
tion."

SOUND EFFECT: Horns honking in a traffic jam,
screech of tires and crashing metal.

ANNOUNCER: Worried about parking? Forget it.
Walk to friendly Wrigley Field. You'll receive absolutely
free one disposable tub of hot water to soak your feet in.

Or your head, if you wish. All you have to do is show the blister on your heel—or the hole in your head.

There you are, Cedric Tallis. Free advice—and worth every penny of it. If that doesn't work, Chuck suggests free admission on Arbor Day to anyone accompanied by a potted plant, free admission on Tuesday to anyone named Tuesday, free admission anytime to anyone named Annie Oakley.

Ford Frick's Gopher Ball

Ford Frick isn't the worst commissioner of baseball in history but he's in the photo. I make him no worse than place. He could get up in the last few strides but I don't think anybody can catch Happy Chandler at the wire. He has too long a lead.

What bugs me about Ford is the way he keeps on knocking his own racket. Now, it's Babe Ruth's sacred record he's worried about. A few years ago, when the Dodgers moved west to the Coliseum, he was worried about the crushing effect the left-field screen would have on baseball.

It so happened that a couple of weeks before the Dodgers moved in a crew of collegians had made mincemeat of the lopsided Coliseum dimensions and had stroked a dozen or so home runs in one turn at bat. I'll always remember when someone hit Pee Wee Reese with this electrifying news. Pee Wee just looked his informant in the eye and drawled: "All I want to know is who was pitching and how can I get at him?"

The point is, good baseball men knew the left-field

screen was not going to overturn baseball in a single season
—or even in a lot of them. One who knew was Johnny
Podres, who coolly went out that year and mopped up the
league in the Coliseum by making all the hitters hit to right
where the fence barely made the county line. Johnny
knew a pitchers' paradise when he saw it.

Bob Friend, that same year, told me he felt relieved right
after he saw the screen because he knew it would cost real
sluggers, like Willie Mays, Aaron, or Banks, about six
homers a year—line shots that would turn into singles
crashing into the screen on the way into orbit.

But Ford Frick was on national TV with Red Smith on
the eve of that season agreeing solemnly that some adjust-
ments would have to be made in the record book in case
Ruth's record was broken by—hold on to your hats—Gil
Hodges or Charlie Neal.

Now it's Mantle and Maris that have Ford reaching for
the panic button. Seems the American League season has
expanded to 162 games and, if Mantle or Maris breaks
Ruth's record, Frick means to have him do it in the old
regulation 154 games. Ford drops the flag on the race after
154 games have been played regardless of whether Maris or
Mantle have played 154 up to that time or not. His notion is that Ruth had to hit his sixty in 154 games and
that will be the yardstick. Players of one era should not
get an edge over players of another, is his feeling.

OK, Ford. Let's play that both ways. Let's expunge
Christy Mathewson's records because he could legally
throw the spitball. Let's throw Ty Cobb out of there because he never had to play night ball and any hitter will
tell you night ball has to cost the batter twenty points a
season.

And let's not stop with Mantle or Maris at making them set their records in 154 games. Let's make them duplicate Ruth's record in detail in order to qualify.

For instance, let's once and for all find out if any of Ruth's home runs *did* go in the stands on the bounce— which was a legal home run in those days. Then, let's make Mickey or Roger hit exactly that many home runs on the bounce. Or be disqualified.

Let's make them hit the same number of homers off a spitball that Ruth did. If Ruth hit a home run with a fol- lowing wind of over twenty miles an hour, let's insist that Maris or Mantle do likewise. For every one they don't match, we'll subtract one they hit *into* the wind.

Since Ruth didn't hit any of his home runs at night, let's throw out all the ones his competitors do hit at night.

If investigation proves Ruth hit only one-sixth of his home runs to left field, let's make Roger Maris match that. If he doesn't we'll say, "Sorry, old man, Ruth hit 10 of them to left, you hit only eight. So, we penalize you two home runs and you lose."

The baseball season is now 162 games in the American League, and that is a fact of baseball. Presumably, expan- sion will make it more in years to come. If some batter hits 61 home runs, which is entirely likely the way the Yankees M-Squad is going, *that* is going to be the record as far as baseball is concerned. If it's any comfort to the figure phil- berts, let them sniff that Ruth hit his homers at the rate of every 2.5 games while his successor hit them at the rate of every 2.6 games. (Of course, if Mantle hits sixty-five, they won't even have this hedge.)

That ought to satisfy Frick. If it doesn't he can take his fat pension and retire to become personal custodian of Ruth's record. I have just the man to fill his shoes. Spike Jones.

Percentage Still Rules

The trouble with baseball fans is that they are basically overconservative and change frightens them. I happen to know this because I saw a psychological study made by a firm called Pair, Inc., a year or so ago which noted that people who follow baseball on radio are "very practical, very material, down-to-earth."

They come largely from the ranks of business and professional people and "place a great deal of value on the concrete and specific—not as interested in new adventure or new experiences as others."

I bring this up because I notice that a great many fans are shook up over Cubs owner Phil Wrigley's plan not to hire a manager this year but to run his club with eight coaches and a computer machine.

Please don't panic, folks. In the words of the old Roman philosopher, "The more things change, the more they remain the same." Particularly in baseball.

Let's examine the computer machine first. You might expect it to show some invention at first—like letting the pitcher bat for himself if you haven't got anybody better on the bench, or letting the infield stay deep with a runner on third because you got a catcher who couldn't block the plate against his grandmother.

But with eight old-timers around to advise it, I predict the computer will begin behaving like Walt Alston or Solly Hemus by mid-season. This is to say, it will do the same things in the same way in 1961 that Connie Mack did in 1911.

For instance—

It will jerk a .330 left-handed hitter because there is a left-hander pitching and will replace him with a .230 hitter whose virtue is he's right-handed. The other manager—the live one in the dugout—will counter with a right-handed pitcher. The computer then will order a switch to a left-handed-hitting utility man, batting average .210. This is known in baseball as "playing the percentage," I think because it figures out that the master mind has thought his way out of one hundred percentage points in two moves.

The machine will recommend that Ernie Banks bunt with two men on and no one out because you always bunt in that situation—particularly if the next two men up are in a slump and haven't hit a ball out of the infield even in batting practice in weeks.

When it comes to trimming the roster, the machine will keep the creaky old-timer whose fast ball wouldn't break your teeth if you caught it in the mouth because he's got control. It will let the kid with all the stuff go because he can't get it over the plate even though he's so fast the umpires who need glasses aren't sure if he threw it.

It will send down the free-swinger who led the minors in home runs last year because he strikes out a lot and it will keep the chop-chop hitter to work the hit-and-run play even though the only guy on the club fast enough to make it work is the bat boy.

It will leave the starting pitcher in the day he takes the mound with a hangover and everyone is hitting the ball right on the nose only the outfielders save him with sensational catches—but it will immediately derrick the pitcher with lots of stuff who gets stuck for a handle hit, a pop-fly the first baseman loses in the sun, a ground ball that takes a bad hop and socks the third baseman in the nose, and a passed ball the catcher loses on the third strike.

It will swap jobs with the guy in the radio booth by July. And a good thing, too.

As to why Phil Wrigley wanted eight coaches, I think that's understandable, too. First of all, he probably wanted two tables of bridge. And, if he had more than nine, the coaches—who have to sit down to think—would outnumber the players and the overflow would have to wait outside the dugout. The prospect of Ernie Banks standing between innings would appeal only to the opposing pitcher.

Actually, Phil Wrigley is the kind of man who takes his civic obligations hard. He won't play night baseball in his park, for instance, because he doesn't want to disturb his neighbors. If I had his money, I would play at 2 o'clock in the morning and hire a brass band, if I felt like it, but that's the way he is.

So, it is only natural for him to be as concerned about unemployment as the Administration is. With two platoons of coaches, he is doing his bit for the country and making sure the Cubs draw more people than they did last year.

Of course, there is this to consider: with eight coaches to run the club, there won't be much for each to do. To tell the truth, there isn't enough for one to do. So, with all that time on their hands, these guys figure to chew a lot of gum. This will give other Wrigley employees something to do. The Cubs may turn the tide of recession all by themselves. But they'll still finish in the second division.

"M" for Murder

When he was only one day old, Mickey Charles Mantle had a baseball put in his hand by his father. When he was four years old, he had a bat put in his hand. When he was five years old, he began to have curve balls thrown at him.

Mickey Mantle has been a ballplayer all his life. Oddly enough, it has never been clearly established he wanted to be. The pay is good, the hours can't be beat, but the central fact is Mickey had no freer choice than a kid who's led down a coal mine in his first pair of long pants.

Mickey's father had the best of intentions. It was precisely to escape the zinc mines of Commerce, Oklahoma, where he spent his own life, that he thrust baseball on his son.

In 1946, Mickey had to plead to be allowed to try football. His father relented. The result was a shin bruise in a pileup which was to affect his entire life. When it swelled alarmingly, a specialist was consulted. "You have osteomyelitis," he told Mickey.

The strange story of Mickey Mantle's career after that shattering incident is told in a revealing biography by Dick Schaap, *Mickey Mantle, the Indispensable Yankee*, an indispensable book.

No one brought more inborn talent to the big leagues than Mickey Mantle. He was a switch hitter because his father made him. He was a hitter because nature made him. Yet there were times when he wept with frustration and wanted to quit. His father, of course, wouldn't let him.

When Mickey appeared in the Yankee training camp in

Arizona in 1951, the sportswriters pulled out all the stops. Ty Cobb had been born again. The journalist, Tom Meany, surveyed this chorus of praise in some amazement and then suggested perhaps Mantle skip playing altogether and "go straight to Cooperstown and get in a glass cage."

There were some doctors who thought it might be a fine idea. Osteomyelitis, it happens, is an infection of the bone marrow which can be controlled but rarely cured. A membrane like the inner covering of an egg covers up the infection giving the appearance of healing. But any jar or bruise breaks it open again. Baseball is not the happiest environment for a man carrying its bacteria around with him.

For an ordinary mortal, Mantle's ten-year achievements in baseball—.307 lifetime average, 993 runs batted in, 323 home runs, 1611 base hits—are perfectly astonishing. For a man with osteomyelitis, they are incredible.

Yet, it is a melancholy fact that Yankee fans ring each other up on game day at the Stadium with a bright idea: "Let's go out and boo Mantle." He has been upbraided by his own manager, riddled by the press, and even a rival manager, Al Lopez, who should have been glad of it, was moved once to mourn "Mickey Mantle is the most talented natural ballplayer I've ever seen but he hasn't fully capitalized on his gifts."

Part of the trouble is Mantle keeps coming up with mysterious leg injuries which are always explained away in terms of the familiar sprains, tears, and Charley horses all baseball is prey to. Forgotten is the fact that some doctors, on the first outbreak of Mickey's bone disease, counseled amputation as a hedge against a painful late life—or even an absence of one.

Mickey has seldom said anything—not even when he

takes the field with a limp and the inflammatory words "dogging it" get thrown around loosely.

He has continued to play superior baseball—and kept his problems to himself. When I discussed his disease with him, Mickey only said "It's arrested now. I don't think about it."

Once, when a group of Dodgers were heaping some coal on the legend of Mantle's apparent indifference, Jackie Robinson broke up the discussion by noting quietly, "Look, we got plenty of guys worse than he is. Trouble is, we ain't got anybody as good."

Mickey's burden with the Yankees was that he was replacing Joe DiMaggio—virtually alone. The Yankees had always had its assassins in tandem—Ruth and Gehrig, Gehrig and DiMaggio, DiMaggio and Keller. DiMag quit when Mickey was a pup.

Mickey now has an accomplice. Roger Maris. It puts the pressure on a pitcher. Both benefit. And the press box is alive with alliteration. Mantle and Maris have become "Dial M for Murder," "Murder and Mayhem," "Maul and Mangle," and, in the words of Eli Grba, who has to get them out, "Thunder and Lightning." Around the league, the managers term them "Messrs. Assault and Battery."

In 1927, Ruth and Gehrig broke the record for home runs by teammates when Babe hit 60 and Gehrig 47. I asked Mickey in the dressing room what the chances were for the M-Squad.

Mickey grinned. "Yeah, I read about that." He turned to Maris. "We should do it, Rog—if you get 70." "I was counting on you," countered Maris.

Funny thing is, they both could be right.

Pun My Word

Sarcasm, it is said, is the lowest form of wit. But, even so, puns have to look up to it. My puns are half-baked but not hot or cross. And served up for the groaning bored.

It all started with Art Seidenbaum ruminating (an old English expression not to be confused with eating in your room) that as long as the New York Mets had signed Elio Chacon to play shortstop, they should scout around for a first baseman named Gout (pronounced "Goo") so they could announce a ground-out as "Chacon a son Gout."

Then, of course, that set me to thinking that if the Pirates' Dick Groat got thrown out stealing, would you say the catcher got his Groat?

And if catcher Don Leppert wiped mud off his pants after a slide, you would have to admit that the Leppert was changing his spots.

I have been waiting all year for Tim Harkness to hit a home run in the thirteenth inning for the Dodgers so we could say the game was called on account of Harkness. And if someone slid back to first under a tag by Tim, you could accurately report he got back safely under cover of Harkness.

Should the rooters of Jerry Lynch be known as a Lynch mob? If Joe Gaines got a home run would manager Fred Hutchinson say "That's capital, Gaines!" But if he registered only a single the next time, you would have to report that Gaines dropped fractionally.

If the Dodgers knocked Joe Gibbon out of the box, would you say they made a monkey out of Gibbon? Or would Gibbon go ape? There are days when Bob doesn't look too Purkey. And others when Jim looks like a lot of Maloney.

When someone brought a rabbit stew to the Reds' clubhouse and Fred Hutchinson ate most of the meat out of it, Frank Robinson came in hungry and said, "Where's the rabbit?" And they naturally said "In the Hutch."

Whenever Hank Foiles hits one out, do rival managers shout "Curses, Foiles again!"?

When Johnny Roseboro knocks Felix Mantilla down sliding into third, don't you have to say he laced Mantilla? If the Phillies decide to keep Reuben Amaro out of the line-up, do they explain that "Amaro is another day." Of course, Amaro may be too late and, if so, does the manager say, "I'll cry, Amaro"?

If the Orioles' Marv Breeding wins a game with a homer, you have to call it a triumph of good Breeding. But if he wins one on a base on balls you have to say it was due to selective Breeding. On the other hand, if he squeals on his roomie for coming in late, you must note regretfully that bad Breeding will always tell.

When Norm Larker is called out on strikes and begins kicking helmets and throwing bats in the dugout, does the umpire cup his hand to his ear and say "Hark, Hark, the Larker"? And if he switches to the outfield, does that automatically make him a meadow Larker?

If you get a base on balls off Joey Jay, are you a Jay-walker? And do you have to stand up if the catcher starts to sing "Oh, Jay, can you see?"

I can't wait for Phillies infielder Bobby Wine to get a few years on him so we can compare some other twilight veteran to him and say "He's aging like old Wine." When Larry Sherry gives up a home run to Henry Aaron, would you say he's cooking Sherry? But if Larry gets farmed to Richmond, he can always say "Sherry me back to old Virginny." Meanwhile, Birdie Tebbetts is singing "Aaron You Glad You're You?"

When Frank Howard knocks a ball off the foul pole and it's fielded by Wally Post, you have to know he knocked it from pillar to Post. If Pete Richert is being groomed for Sandy Koufax's role in the starting rotation, does that make him a reasonable Koufaxsimile?

Billy Klaus can boot a ground ball and become a veritable Santa Klaus but if Larry Burright throws to the wrong base, the manager has to conclude he's not too Burright. If the Phillies' Ted gets a hit, he's a noble Savage, but, if he strikes out, can even music soothe the Savage breast?

And, finally (and aren't you glad?) if Frank Robinson loafs on a ground single and gets thrown out, do the fans look at each other and say "Why did Robinson cruise so?" Any catcher who has a passed ball on Yankee pitcher Marshall Bridges is burning his Bridges behind him. And in the old days before he was married, wouldn't any female fan of Gene Oliver's be known as Oliver's Twist? If you know them socially you can have a martini with Olivers but if not, you have to tell the bartender you'll have a martini, but leave out the Olivers.

The Junk Dealer

Back in the days before everybody knew it, Jim Brosnan always used to tell me Stu Miller was the best pitcher in baseball. "With his stuff, he's got to be the best just to be in the big leagues at all," Jim explained. "He doesn't dare make a mistake out there."

The last time I looked Miller hadn't. Just ask the American League. His feat of striking out Mantle, Howard and Sievers with the winning run on base in the All-Star game has to rank with—if not outrank—Carl Hubbell's stunt of striking out Ruth, Gehrig, Foxx, Simmons, and Cronin in a row in 1934. After all, Hubbell had a fast ball.

Stu Miller in the big leagues is like a boy walking through Indian country with a Boy Scout knife and his lunch in a bag. "He's got a fast ball you could catch in your teeth," is the baseball catch-phrase for it. He's got three speeds of pitches—slow, slower and reverse. When the wind is blowing out, there is a good chance the ball won't get there at all.

In 1934, when Hubbell was mastering the American League in an All-Star game in the Polo Grounds, baseball legend recalls that Lou Gehrig, after swinging lustily at Hubbell's low-ball wizardry, whispered to Jimmy Foxx on his way out of the batter's box, "You might as well swing, it won't get any higher." With Miller, the word is "You might as well wait. It won't get any faster."

To hit Stu Miller a batter needs the patience of a guy waiting for his wife to get dressed to go out. He's the only guy in the game who can throw a change-up off a slow ball. His trick is to make the hitter think the ball is coming five minutes before it does. Around the league, they are waiting for the day some eager rookie gets *two* swings at the same pitch. "Miller," Broz told me, "will strike out some kid on two pitches some night."

There are pitfalls. With a ball like Miller's that finds its way to the plate like a kid on his way to take a bath on Saturday night, there is danger a runner like Willie Davis could steal second base on the trot. But Miller himself is unwilling to admit his fast-ball could pass for a change-up with any other pitcher. "I think I've got a very good fast ball," he told me in the Coliseum the other night. "I'll tell you something. I couldn't even throw this hard a few years ago. I'm getting faster."

The Dodgers' Jim Gilliam is one who agrees. "He seems pretty quick," acknowledges Jim. "Of course, it looks even faster on top of all that slow stuff."

Gilliam, who prides himself he can wait for a strike even if it won't get here until tomorrow, points out: "Miller has more effect on a slugger than a guy like me. I mean, he'll get me out and I'll get my hits off him. But he tries to make you chase. And if you're a big swinger or a guess hitter, you're overmatched." Adds Gilliam: "If you take your head off the ball you're dead."

Duke Snider is one who admits Miller can hypnotize a big swinger. "The ball is always doing something and he's always doing something. He jerks his head or waves his mitt and you're striding before the ball is halfway there."

For Stu Miller, the game of baseball is a cat-and-mouse game. And he's the mouse. It is up to him to con big strong-backed swingers into expending their swing a split second before they've got anything to expend it on. It's the most fascinating show in baseball today, like watching a man stave off a starving lion with a knife and fork.

What Miller does is perfectly legal but it has the effect of a rank balk in which he pretends to throw the ball but doesn't. He was asked if he ever felt like laughing when he saw some slugger swing so hard he fell down at a ball that didn't go by him until he was already in the dust. "No," he said, "I'm too busy thinking what I'm going to throw next time."

For Miller, pitching is as exciting as chess. In 73 innings he's allowed only 22 runs and has struck out 57. Striking out that many batters with a ball that comes up like a bottle floating on water has to be the baseball equivalent of winning the National Open with a bag of clubs with no woods in it.

Miller is so good, the Giants' Alvin Dark admits his team has come to over-rely on him. When he pitched in nine out of ten games recently, Dark intercepted him on the way out of the club house and told him, "Go put your clothes on, and get up in the stands. I want this team to get along without you for one night." Rumor has it Stu went up in the seats, bought a bag of popcorn, and when he flipped a quarter to the vendor, the fellow grabbed too soon, fell on his nose and got traded to Coca-Cola.

Horrors, Howard!

Watching Frank Howard come out of the Dodger dugout to start a game is like watching the opening scene of a horror movie. You know the bit: There's an explosion under a polar ice cap some place, the earth rumbles and opens up, and out of it comes this Thing.

It is wearing a frown and blinks in the light as its head comes into view. It starts down toward civilization with giant strides—a mountain with legs—and women scream, men panic, whole cities flee in terror. It walks in the water and the displacement floods half of New York. It comes out on land and crashes into tall buildings, toppling them like a child's blocks. The Army is called out, the United Nations meets in emergency session and they begin to fire bombs at it, which it catches and throws back.

This, in a way, is Howard marching through baseball, a monster, hip-deep in a crowd of ordinary mortals he is innocently bruising. He hits a home run and a teammate reaches out to shake hands with him—and a moment later lets out a scream of pain. A pitcher fires a high, inside fast ball and the next thing he knows he is down on his hands and knees groping in the grass for the ball—also for his glasses and teeth.

Thus, Frank Howard is in many ways a legend before his own time. But just like the movie prehistoric monster, which always proves to have some simple vulnerability like a head cold, or girls. Howard has his—a breaking ball low and outside. Catchers and umpires have to move back when Frank is swinging at one of these. The swish of the bat is like the falling of a large tree.

When he gets a hit, his gallop to first base is a graceful thing to watch—like the lead buffalo in a stampede. The infielder who takes the throw mentally reviews his insurance program. Some night, Howard is going to run over a second baseman and they are going to have to dig up half the infield because they will not know which is dirt and which is the second baseman.

Howard's idea of hustle is to tear ahead like Alan (The Horse) Ameche on the 2-yard line at Green Bay. They told him about Enos Slaughter being such a hustler he always beat the rest of the club in the dugout at the end of the inning even though he had to come in from right field. Howard got the idea. Only he can't beat anybody in because the rest of the club gets the hell out of the way, when they hear those No. 14s coming.

If determination will make a ballplayer, a proposition

that is open to serious question, Howard will have the game of baseball yelling for help before long.

He is so pathetically anxious to succeed that sometimes it makes your heart ache to see Stu Miller or Lew Burdette toying with him. Then, next thing you know, he has smashed the ball in the general direction of Canada and you feel sorry for *them*. They have the look on their face of a guy who has just stuck his finger in an electric socket he thought was disconnected.

Howard smashed a line drive in Cincinnati last week that lifted outfielder Vada Pinson right off his feet. He was lucky it didn't carry him over the wall with it. When Howard really meets the ball, they don't need a tape measure, they need an aerial survey.

In the outfield, regrettably, Howard is right out of the Marx Brothers. Going after a fly ball, he looks like a moose chasing a butterfly. He can put more suspense into catching a routine fly than Alfred Hitchcock can put into a chase over rooftops.

Frank admits it himself. In a burst of candor which may get him run out of an industry which not only doesn't think honesty is the best policy, it doesn't even put it in the first 10, Howard says, "I really butcher that outfield."

But there is no pitcher in the league who can honestly say he is glad to see this mass of muscle come to bat. Even blindfolded, Howard would make a pitcher's palms sweat. At 6 feet 7 inches, 250 pound Frank looks as if he should be brought to the plate by a gantry and have an astronaut in his cap.

His strike zone is so big, it should be sub-divided. He led the team in strikeouts last year and saw so many balls across the knees he got a crick in the neck looking for them. But he also led the team in home runs.

He is an uncertain base runner. He goes down to first base in three strides and when he lands on the bag they usually have to excavate it before continuing.

But, once on base, he hears voices. In Milwaukee the other night, they belonged to Eddie Mathews and Joe Adcock. "Go back, go back." "Take a lead, take a lead," they counseled him. Frank got as spooky as an old maid who forgot to look under the bed.

Yet, Howard is having a fine year and is almost the key man on the Dodgers at the moment, on a team so platoon-happy it is doubtful if Babe Ruth would get to find out whether he could hit left-handed pitching. Frank is the nearest thing to a bona-fide cleanup hitter and it is melancholy to find Howard platooned out of a game in the ninth inning when the team suddenly needs a home run like eyes but finds itself with the double-play platoon.

On another score, Frank is as refreshing to baseball as the seventh-inning stretch. On an average of three mornings a week on a road trip, the place to get Howard's autograph is at church. Even when the team pulls into town at 3 o'clock in the morning, the first thing Frank studies in the lobby is the church directory. He converted to Catholicism when he married his pretty wife Carol and he takes his belief in God as dedicatedly as he does everything else.

In the lobby of a Milwaukee hotel, Frank spoke—typically—not of what he wanted out of baseball but what he wanted to put into it. "It looks like an easy game. It isn't. I suppose I could have gotten discouraged and taken my bonus money and gone through the motions. But rather than sit around and mope, I would rather go out and work. You know, it's a kind of sad game when you figure there are twenty-five guys who would give their right arm to play and only nine can make it. It is a privilege to be one of the nine."

Frank has been given more pieces of advice than a new widow with a large inheritance. If he could use one more it would be this: Don't change. Baseball needs Frank Howard more than vice versa. If he doesn't make it, I don't want to be the one who has to explain it to the kids.

The first time you lay eyes on Frank Howard, you have to resist the temptation to look behind him to see where you wind it up.

Frank Howard is so big, he wasn't born, he was founded. He's only two stories shorter than the Istanbul Hilton. When he falls asleep on an airplane, which he does all the time, he has to bend his knees. Either that, or hang landing lights on his feet.

He's the most awesome public monument this side of Mt. Rushmore. It would take a fly a week to walk across his wrists. Mickey Rooney can only communicate with him by phone. He's Gulliver in a baseball suit. If he shakes hands with you, you have to call a plumber to get loose. And Blue Cross has an automatic cancellation clause if he slaps you on the back. You get the feeling he's not actually a man, just an unreasonable facsimile.

When you see him walk down the street, you half expect to see Dr. Frankenstein in close pursuit wearing a worried look and a net and explaining to police that one of his experiments got out of hand and also out of the laboratory. "Did you see something go by here with nuts and bolts sticking out of his forehead, er, kind of clanked when it walked?" he will ask. "He's about 7 ft. tall, weighs more than the Mauretania and will probably be found trying to play right field."

Any town not prepared for Frank Howard is apt to declare martial law. He could empty a bar quicker than an angry wife if he ever went in one which he doesn't. If he put an earring in his ear and got a closer haircut he could get rich cleaning frying pans. He makes every other man in the world look like Manners, the butler. He's such a big eater, the smaller players on the team won't sit down at the same table with him. Frank's liable to plunge a fork in them and wash them down with a bottle of ketchup before they can call for help.

He leads the major leagues in one-handed home runs. He takes one hand off the bat before he swings otherwise he will atomize the ball. Even when he bunts, the stitches fly off. The third-base coach is covered by a special floater policy when Howard comes to bat. Leo Durocher gives him signals from left field and one night Maury Wills got to third, then saw Frank Howard at bat and stole second. Anyone who stops a Frank Howard line drive wears a patch over his eye or has a credit card with his neighborhood brain surgeon. He has made third base such an unpopular position that the only people who will play it in the future are convicted murderers and would-be suicides.

Pitchers throw him slow stuff so they will have plenty of time to run and hide. The last guy to throw Frank Howard a fast ball has been in a state of nervous shock ever since. The left fielder got out of the way just in time or he would have had a hole in him five and a half inches in diameter.

Frank is so strong he can only grip the bat with three fingers of each hand. He's got a great throwing arm, but it's so long he picks up the ball in right field but doesn't let go of it until first base.

He got $108,000 to play baseball from the Dodgers,

rumor has it, because they had to outbid two house-wrecking teams who wanted to use Frank for slum clearance. He could knock down more buildings than a crane with an iron ball on the end of it.

When Frank Howard runs in from right field, seismologists as far away as Johannesburg phone the ball park in panic as they record an earthquake of the first magnitude on the Richter scale. If he berthed his shoes on the waterfront, the longshoremen would go on strike. Shoeshine boys shine them in shifts.

He swung at so many bad pitches when he first came up that the manager had to plead with him to wait until Stu Miller at least threw the ball. He had two strikes on him one night while Stu was still at the rosin bag. He's much better now. He only takes one swing at the rosin bag.

If he didn't make good, he might have thrown the country into a Depression. Walter O'Malley paid so much money for him that he began to think he should have bought the British Empire instead. "Will he make good?" I asked Walter in the spring of 1958 as the owner was busy planting some meta-sequoia trees which didn't make good either and were as long gone as Clint Hartung by the All-Star break. "If he doesn't, you're going to see the damnedest unemployment since the bank holiday," O'Malley promised.

Most people, if they get $108,000, would head right for the French Riviera on the double and wouldn't even let Stu Miller pass them the sugar. But Frank Howard is as stubborn as alimony.

If he sees two more movies he will beat Hedda Hopper's lifetime average by one. His taste runs to shoot-em-ups and he has clocked more gunfire than the German army in his young life. He answers to the nickname "Hondo" because

he's the only guy in the world outside of organized basketball who could call John Wayne "Shorty." He has seen
every Indian John Wayne ever killed. He won't let anybody
tell him the plot even of movies he's seen before.

When Frank charges from first to third on a hit, a freeway
sigalert is sounded because if anyone gets in his way he
will kill more people than Labor Day traffic. He pays no
more attention to signals than a bison frightened by lightning and one night when Lee Walls put the sign on for a
squeeze play and dashed home only to see Frank step into
a pitch and swing mightily, he fainted dead away. They
had to revive him to tag him out. But if Frank had met
the ball he would not only have been a corpse, he would
have been a toothless one. There would have been eyeglasses and teeth all the way to third base.

Baseball always makes the Frank Howards work twice
as hard and wait twice as long to play regularly. A manager,
you must understand, can never recall home runs as clearly
as strikeouts. Lou Gehrig may have been the second-great-
est player in the history of the game, but he had to stand
in line behind a chorus of banjo hitters because the
manager thought he swung at too many bad pitches. The
fact he knocked those bad pitches off the centerfield loud-
speakers impressed nobody but the pitcher who tried to
waste that pitch.

Howard is the closest thing to Lou Gehrig in devotion,
modesty, perseverance and raw strength the game has ever
seen. It almost took an act of Congress to put him in the
regular lineup. But it will take an act of God to get him
out as it did Gehrig. And Frank Howard is on very good
terms with the Lord, as was Lou. If he's not in a movie,
he's in a church.

He's a very good person, but that's not the reason no

one in the league will pick a fight with him. When a home plate battle starts and big Frank comes rumbling in from right field, even the Dodgers scatter. Frank can see pretty well, but if he pulls back his hand to swing at an enemy, the draft can knock over three bystanders.

There's so much of him, it's hard not to throw him a strike. But there isn't a pitcher in the league who wouldn't contribute to a fund to put him on Mars, where they won't believe him either.

Sandy Rare Specimen

For Sanford Koufax, left-handed pitcher, the 1961 baseball season opened on an unusual note—with the manager pounding on his door at 2 o'clock in the morning demanding to be let in at once.

This was unusual because the manager usually wasn't out after curfew. Neither, ordinarily, was Sandy Koufax but this was a night both long shots came in. Well after curfew, as it happens.

The next high spot in Sandy Koufax' banner year came one August night in the Coliseum when he was batting against the Reds' Bob Purkey. Sandy swung at a thrown ball—and expected to miss it as usual. Instead, the ball rocketed out to right field.

Koufax stood there for a moment. Then he looked around to see who did it. By this time, his teammates were on their feet in the dugout waving their hats and pointing frantically to first base. Sandy set sail. But in the outfield,

Frank Robinson casually picked up his base hit and threw him out at first.

The tragic part of that is that if Sandy Koufax had gotten that hit, he would be batting .077 today instead of .062.

Sandy Koufax is not exactly a character invented by Al Capp. But he is a rare specimen for baseball. In a game where the vocabulary runs to four-letter words and the vocal range registers from loud to hoarse, Sandy is articulate and soft-spoken. Where the musical tastes run to rock'n roll or hill-billy gut-bucket, Sandy prefers Mendelssohn and Beethoven. Where plenty of players only act like bachelors, Sandy is one. And doesn't act like it.

Where teammates seek out the nearest cowboy picture, Sandy looks for the foreign art film. Where other players' raiment make them look as though they're trying to be sure the deer hunters see them, Sandy's is subdued—but expensive. There are those who think Sandy's salary just pauses briefly in his pocket on the way to the alpaca sweater industry. On road trips, Sandy can be found either at the ball park or in a men's store. He stands in line waiting for them to open in the morning and some suspect he asks for autographs of the owners whose stock he most admires.

Sandy Koufax didn't even particularly want to be a ballplayer. He went to Cincinnati University on a basketball scholarship and had not even played a great deal of baseball on the streets of Brooklyn where he grew up. Sandy wanted to be an architect and there are still days when he feels he has made a terrible mistake—almost as if Frank Lloyd Wright had decided to become a rodeo rider.

The trouble was, Sandy Koufax was such a natural pitcher baseball couldn't afford to let him turn to mere bridge-building. Sandy's fast ball was so fast, some batters would start to swing as he was on his way to the mound. His curve ball disappeared like a long putt going in a hole.

Koufax has never pitched an inning of minor-league ball which doesn't make him unique but makes him a member of a very small club. As a result, he has learned his craft slowly. And it's as exasperating as hay fever: one day you have it, the next day you don't. Sandy thinks it is basically a problem of rhythm. You don't know till you hear the music of the first pitch smacking in the catcher's glove—or off the center-field fence—whether you're going to dance or trip over your feet.

The Dodgers have persevered a long time with Sandy Koufax. On the other hand, he has given baseball lots of second chances, too, when you consider the building boom in this country. Players who have batted against him have been waiting confidently for him to elbow Lefty Grove to one side in the Hall of Fame.

This year, both have had their patience rewarded. Koufax has not only won fifteen games, a personal high, but he was the man who caught the falling Dodgers on the way down the side of a cliff and held them by their heels till they could scramble to the second place ledge. If Koufax hadn't defeated Cincinnati last Friday his team would now be as far out of it as the *Andrea Doria*.

When they dropped a double-header and came into Chicago like a drowning man with a rock in his lap, Koufax pitched a virtual no-hitter. A catchable fly ball and a half-hit ground ball to right field represented the entire offensive thrust of the Chicago Cubs for the afternoon. A good thing, because the Dodgers didn't make anybody forget the 1927 Yankees either.

Koufax has struck out so many batters, he is approaching records set by pitchers in the pre-historic ages of baseball like Rube Marquard and someone named "Noodles" Hahn. He is a victim of his own stuff—he averaged 155 pitches a game last year, largely because batters get so little wood on the ball they can't even pop it up and foul it back instead. He has fanned 895 batters in 898 innings.

Sandy is now sure he wants to stay in baseball. And the batters wish he'd go build something. Success may go to his pocketbook—or to Hart, Schaffner & Marx. But it won't go to his head. Joe Frisco once said of Irving Berlin that he had a nice voice but you had to hug him to hear it. With Koufax even that wouldn't help. When Sandy is shouting, he sounds as if he is talking to himself.

When the Dodgers get to Chavez Ravine, Sandy Koufax may finally put the game of baseball on the run. He has won nine, lost two on the road, won six, lost seven in the Coliseum. Even if he does rout the record book, you will never know by looking at him. He will be the nice young man with the gentle brown eyes standing in the corner looking as though he had come in for autographs.

Wonderful Willie

The first thing to establish about Willie Mays is that there really is one.

He's 5 ft. 10, weighs 183, has five fingers on each hand, five toes on each foot, two eyes, all his teeth, and a nice smile. He's quite mortal. He makes $90,000 a year but gets to keep only enough to pay off the alimony and the rent on time and is made up like the rest of us of about 87 cents worth of iron, calcium, antimony and of whatever baser metal a human being is composed of. Only in his case, it's put together a little better than the rest of us.

All this is important to know in talking to baseball people because when you mention Willie Mays, several things happen: a film comes over their eyes, their cheeks flush and flecks of foam appear at the corners of their mouths. Listening to them, you half expect to see the Angel Gabriel running around with No. 24 on his back. At the very least, you think they are describing one of their own hallucinations—a combination of Babe Ruth, Ty Cobb and Elmer the Great, a comic strip character 28 ft. tall pasted together out of old clippings of *The Sporting News* or conjured out of a pot of re-heated Welsh rarebit.

Willie Mays is so good the other players don't even resent him. They have had his name in standing type in Cooperstown's Hall of Fame ever since he was a rookie. Leo Durocher started to drool the first time he saw Willie Mays and he hasn't stopped since. "If he could cook, I'd marry him," Leo once announced.

The only thing he can't do on a baseball field is fix the plumbing. As a batter, Bill Rigney once said, his only weakness was a wild pitch. But he hit one of those in spring practice for a clean single from a semiprone position. As long as gravity is working, he'll catch any ball hit or thrown in his vicinity. His vicinity is anywhere between the foul lines. Sometimes the leftfielder is instructed to go after only foul balls to keep out of Mays' way.

The only place in the world they boo him is San Francisco. This makes strong men cover their ears because around the rest of the league they consider anyone who would boo Willie Mays would kick in a stained-glass window.

Part of the trouble is that when the Giants transferred

to San Francisco, the press there and in New York gave the impression Willie Mays and the Seven Dwarfs were coming to the Coast with Horace Stoneham and two lame-armed pitchers. They didn't expect Willie Mays to land there; they expected the waters of the Golden Gate to part and let him walk ashore. Or, if he flew, they didn't think he would need an airplane. The first time he struck out there was a gasp as if someone had just let the air out of the town.

It was said his life used to be 95 percent baseball and 5 percent cowboy movies. Then he got married and the ratio went down. His life became only 93 percent baseball.

He can do one more thing than any other great slugger in the history of the game—steal bases. He is the only man in history to hit more than thirty home runs and steal more than thirty bases a season—and he does it habitually.

He has been shy most of his life. He needs constant reassurance. The product of a broken home in Alabama, raised by an aunt, he never takes anything for granted. He doesn't drink or smoke and scandal has never touched his life. He is a credit not to his race but the human race.

Off-field, he is a pleasant, rather lonely young man. He had his thirty-first birthday dinner alone in a St. Louis hotel room with a newspaperman, Harry Jupiter, of the San Francisco *Examiner*. In spring training, he was a frequent dinner guest of a bus boy on the base. So far as is known he has never done an unkind thing in his career—except hit four home runs in one day off Milwaukee pitchers. That's as many as anyone ever hit in one 9-inning stretch.

He is modest. When he was with Minneapolis in 1951 and a Giant official got on the phone to send for him after the Giants had just lost eleven games in a row, Willie demurred. "I'm not ready, yet, I'm not coming," he protested. "What are you batting?" the official asked. ".477," Willie answered. There was a thud on the other end of the line as the man fainted.

The Giants won the pennant that year but Willie went hitless his first twenty-two times at bat. Manager Leo Durocher came upon him in the clubhouse. Tears were streaming down Willie's cheeks. "I can't help it. I can't hit them cats, Mistah Leo," he sobbed. Leo put his arm around him. "I brought you up here to play centerfield. You are the greatest centerfielder I have ever seen, probably that the game has ever seen. Get out there and play it!"

Willie Mays did. The first pitch the next day—off Warren Spahn—he put over the roof. He's been doing it ever since. "I think I'll steal less from now on," he told me Tuesday night, "because I hope I can play for ten years more." I got news for him: baseball hopes so, too.

Nice Guy Also Wins

The scene is any dressing room in the big leagues as the losing team files in after the game. Their leader is a grown man but for the moment he doesn't act like it. It is possible in the mind's eye to see him as he picks up a bench, hurls it at a locker, then throws himself against the wall and hammers on it and curses and sobs.

This is known as "being a tough competitor." Believe it or not.

The scene now shifts to the dressing room of the Chicago White Sox. Coming off a winning streak of nineteen in twenty-two games, they have just been clobbered by a team that at the time has plumbed a depth never before recorded in modern major league history—tenth place.

The manager sits there affably, feet up on the desk, open bottle of beer in hand. He looks up as this reporter enters and a slow grin spreads over his features. "What went wrong, Al?" comes the banal question. With the foot-stool throwers this would open the flood gates to five minutes of ear-scorching profanity that would do justice to a ferry-boat captain. But Al Lopez shrugs. "We got beat," he suggests. "That fellow's got a good curve ball."

Alfonso Ramón Lopez, the Castilian from Tampa, is a gentleman who comes from a long line of them and not even the pressures of pennant baseball can force him to forget the facts. He is the living refutation of the Leo Durocher dictum "nice guys finish last." And it is the hope of everyone who wishes that baseball, despite its business aspects, can somehow keep a semblance of sportsmanship alive, that Al Lopez never does finish last. Everyone now knows those are not nine Frank Merriwells out there in the livery of the home team. But it is to be hoped that they are not nine Attilas the Hun either.

Al Lopez is a manager who has never finished lower than 3rd in his entire career—and that only once. The New York Yankees have lost the pennant only twice in the last twelve years—and Al Lopez managed the team that beat them both times. Whenever he didn't win, he finished second every year but last.

He won the first pennant the Chicago White Sox had won in forty years. You still rub your eyes when you contemplate it. In a power league, his "power" consisted of a sore-backed National League castoff, Ted Kluszewski, and he only had him for the final weeks of the season. His star player was a tobacco-chewing second baseman, Nellie Fox, who has hit a grand total of 29 home runs in twelve years.

His pitching staff consisted of Early Wynn and a bunch of guys fighting control or a sore arm. The team was so creaky it had to be dismantled the next year and then many of its members waived out of town or put up for draft. It seems fairly evident Lopez's record of finishing first or second for twelve years and third for one is about to take the pipe.

But it seemed even more evident earlier this year when the Sox were in the sub-basement and feeling around for a crack of light to find the way out. It is a matter of record the good Señor never kicked a water cooler, cracked a locker door, or threw himself on the floor kicking and screaming. He concentrated on his pitchers instead and for the month of June the Sox were unbeatable.

The talent was too thin for that success to continue indefinitely and the White Sox are once more sifting down toward the bottom of the barrel. If it upsets Lopez, it doesn't show in sarcasm, snarls or sulks. When he relieves his starting pitchers he still acts as though it's going to hurt him more than it does them—unlike a Fred Hutchinson whose hurlers usually put their guard up when they see him coming.

"I don't think blowing your stack helps one damn bit," Lopez asserts. "You waste energy you might better use in thinking. It's not that easy a game that you can tear yourself and your team apart. I take the position everyone is trying his best and the player feels worse than you do when he can't bring that run over or get the side out.

"I remember at Cleveland we lost a tough one once and I just sat in front of the locker and stared. I was stunned. Bob Lemon came over and said, 'Lope, if you'd only *say* something. The guys can't stand it if you won't even talk to them.' That shook me out of it in a hurry. I was letting them down, not them letting me down."

It is an attitude that explains why the Cleveland players bought "Lope" a set of golf clubs when he was forced to resign. It may even explain why the team slipped from second to sixth after he left.

Pass the Potatoes

The biggest eater I ever knew was not an athlete at all but a mere girl, the singer, Rosemary Clooney. The only expense account I ever had challenged was the night I took Rosie to dinner for an interview.

It would have been cheaper to take the Harlem Globetrotters. The food she ate, in the order of its appearance—and disappearance—included: an antipasto; appetizer of mozzarella poured over a paste; minestrone soup; plate of lasagna; veal parmigiana; chocolate eclair; dish of sherbet, and a couple of after-dinner drinks called "capecchino" which consisted of rum, brandy, creme de cocoa, chocolate and whipped cream. It tasted—and counted—like a 100-proof sundae.

Rosie topped this off with a pizza. I was green when I stumbled out of the restaurant but she was still hungry. And she never gained a pound. "Rosie," explained her husband, José Ferrer, "could spot Diamond Jim Brady two pork chops and catch him in the stretch."

The late Joe Palmer's champion was a horse trainer named "Fatty" Anderson. Fatty went up against the champion eater of Cuba once and, as Joe told it, dozens of chickens and hundreds of oysters later, the Cuban was on the ropes on his second apple pie. Anderson ate his placidly and then, when he was through, reached over the table, speared the piece left by his opponent. He hesitated a minute, then called the waiter. He wanted a piece of cheese on it.

Rosie and Fatty were in a class by themselves. But their competition today would come from the world of baseball. Babe Ruth, of course, was the all-time trencherman. His stomach used to rumble in the outfield if the other team had a big inning. They carried him off the train once in Asheville, North Carolina, with the world's most monumental stomach ache and, when Babe was conscious enough to admit it, it developed he had breakfasted on a dozen hot dogs and six bottles of pop that day.

Steve Bilko is commonly believed to hold the free-style hot dog championship of the Coliseum press box—nine in a regulation game. But Steve, like Ruth, has always functioned best on a full stomach. Some feel his career may have been aborted at the start by the Cardinals who used to insist their players weigh in before every game and take a fine for each pound overweight.

Bilko used to beat the rap by plugging the bathroom doors and windows with Turkish towels and turning on the hot water taps full force. You could always tell Bilko's hotel room because the wallpaper would be steamed off the walls and the carpets would be too hot to walk on barefoot.

Leon Wagner's vote goes to Willie McCovey. When they were teammates on the Giants, Wagner invited McCovey to his apartment where Mrs. Wagner would fry up a dozen pork chops for the three of them. The second time McCovey came over, he brought a gift—another dozen pork chops.

The Dodgers' Frank Howard is a growing boy who got $108,000 to sign up but teammate Norm Larker is on record as fearing that won't keep Frank in groceries another year. At Green Bay one night Howard polished off a steak, a banana split, a strawberry sundae, two malted milks and a piece of cake—then got on the bus carrying a gallon of ice cream and a spoon. On plane trips, the Dodgers order sixty steaks for thirty-five passengers. Frank Howard disposes of his like aspirin tablets.

Size has little to do with it. Albie Pearson can eat even up with his roommate, Ted Kluszewski, and once, on the road, Albie asked Klu to order him a glass of orange juice in the restaurant, he would be right down. When he got there, he found a quart of orange juice—on a high-chair.

Kluszewski likes to bake cakes, preferably at one o'clock in the morning when the television gets dull, his wife Eleanor admits. The frosting looks like a box of chocolates that's been left in the sun.

The favorites of Joe Falls, Detroit sportswriter, were Tiger players J. W. Porter and Boots Poffenberger. Porter would climb on a diner stool and order "a dozen eggs over easy." Poffenberger, who got most of his calories out of a bottle, used to telephone room service in the morning and order "a breakfast of champions." "Cereal?" guessed the clerk. "Hell, no," roared Poffenberger. "Two fried eggs and a bottle of beer."

Early Wynn puts ketchup on his flapjacks. Zoilo Versalles ate nothing but cornflakes his first two days in organized ball. Satchel Paige, who used to shoot his own jackrabbits for nourishment in his early days and had to munch soggy hamburgers on draughty busses for most of his barnstorming career, had a tougher fight with his stomach than he did with enemy batters.

He left the writer, Dick Donovan, with a deathless piece of dietary advice: "Avoid fried meats which angry up the blood, and if your stomach disputes you, lie down and pacify it with cool thoughts."

Diet has had some impact. I have seen athletes pile their plates high with chicken, lamb chops and cold cuts and then murmur "Protein. I'm on a diet."

Hap Felton once remembered the pitcher Billy Loes didn't buy it. "If it doesn't make you fat, how come cows are so fat?" he wanted to know. Pee Wee Reese looked at him innocently. "Because they drink all that milk, Billy," he told him.

Home with Brosnan

The trouble with inviting a pitcher out to your house is the effect it has on your family.

Like the other night. I invited Jim Brosnan, the Cincinnati pitcher, out for a relaxing evening of steaks and gin after the Sunday game at the Coliseum.

I carefully briefed the family on how to behave in the presence of a relief pitcher. "He's sick of talking baseball," I warned. "He spends all day in the bull-pen talking baseball."

Ricky, my pre-little leaguer, was puzzled. "With bulls?" he asked.

Ricky doesn't really know much about baseball. He's only eight. He knows only one ballplayer by name—Sandy Koufax. He latched onto him the usual way—bubble-gum cards. Actually, Ricky isn't a baseball fan. He's a bubble-gum fan.

When Broz drove up, Rick was waiting for him. "Are you," he demanded, "as good as Sandy Koufax?" I was furious at this breach of etiquette. "Quiet, Rick," I shouted. "Of course, he isn't."

I made it clear it wasn't as a pitcher I was inviting Brosnan. It's the inner man I warm to—the author. Broz is the only pitcher I know of who thinks of Homer as a Greek poet and not a lucky swing by a banjo hitter. I had in mind an Evening of Culture and Great Books, something Clifton Fadiman might enjoy.

Sody spoiled it first. Sody is cute and blonde, the wife of a psychologist, but she doesn't know anything about baseball. In fact, she wishes they'd put atomic scientists on bubble-gum cards. "I should think," she told Brosnan, "you'd rather be a starting pitcher. Doesn't it get boring sitting around in that cow-pen all day?"

"Not if you bring martinis," Broz told her.

"You don't get a very good view of the game," Sody said accusingly. "That's the best part of it," agreed Brosnan. "Most of the guys would rather watch girls anyway."

Broz was not entirely popular with the oldest boy, Ted, who is, poor devil, a Dodger fan. "If you get in the World Series with the Yankees," he said resentfully, "what do you think will happen?" "They'll blow us right out of the ball-park," answered Brosnan. "Broz," I shouted. "He'll believe you. Quit kidding." Broz looked at me. "Who's kidding?" he asked.

The psychologist didn't believe a ball curved. I said this question has been asked and answered and baseball's position was quite clear, a ringing "the hell it don't curve." Teddy believes a ball curves but that it didn't matter to a good hitter. Like him. We went out in the back yard for the experiment.

"I'll throw a slow curve," announced Brosnan. Teddy went into his crouch, the one he's copied from Stan Musial on television—or bubble gum, I forget which. "Wait a minute," I shouted, just in time.

"Ted, you'll break a window when you hit it." Broz gave me a funny look. "*Roseboro* can't hit this pitch," he said accusingly.

"I know," I shrieked, "but Roseboro's *guessing*. My kid murders slow curves. I mean, Koufax couldn't get him out." Broz looked at me. "Would you like to try to hit it?" he asked evenly. He had a look in his eye for a minute like Don Drysdale. "I gotta go fix a drink," I said and slunk off.

I could see the evening was a cultural shambles. So I decided to ask Broz what had happened in the game that afternoon. "What was the matter with Drysdale?" I asked. "He didn't have good stuff. But his control was excellent," Broz explained.

"Right around the plate?" I guessed. "Right around the head," answered Brosnan.

"You see," he went on, "when you don't have your stuff, you want to get out of there as quick as you can. Now, you can do this in one of two ways. You can toss it up there and let 'em hit it and your manager will get you out of there. Or you can toss it up there and let it hit them. The umpire will get you out of there.

"Drysdale is a curious case," he continued. "I estimate the brushback pitch, which is the polite term for it, is 10 percent of baseball. But some place along the line, Drysdale got the idea it's 90 percent of it. I wouldn't be surprised it's keeping him from being a great pitcher."

"What does your team think about it?" I asked. "We're

having a meeting in the morning," Broz said carefully. "We'll decide then." I suddenly felt a shiver. I pictured one of those meetings Eliot Ness is always breaking up, or a car pulling up as Drysdale was walking out of the Coliseum some night and five Cincinnati Reds leaping out and gunning him down.

"The way Drysdale throws, he might as well throw a grenade with the pin out," added Broz. "You know, Art Mahaffey of the Phils never pitches against us any more. He threw at our guys one night when he got mad. And now, Gene Mauch knows he might as well push him off a bridge as play him against us."

Sody was dismayed. "I didn't think you were supposed to hit people in baseball," she said, shocked. "Couldn't somebody get hurt?" I sighed. "Broz," I asked, "read any good books lately?"

Jack Be Nimble

It took Baseball over fifty years to admit Negroes to our "national" pastime—a fact of life that should make it always hang its head in shame—but I was amused and gratified, both, to note the alacrity with which they admitted Jackie Robinson to the Hall of Fame.

They fell all over themselves because nobody wants to mess with Jackie. If they slammed the door of the Hall of Fame on *him*, he'd kick it in. He'd make it if he had to come in a spike-high slide and some of baseball's most hallowed custodians would have spike wounds from ankle to ear.

And if I were Sid Keener, director at Cooperstown, I'd be very careful where I put the Robinson mementos. Jackie is very sensitive about back seats anywhere.

I have always considered that Jackie Robinson was very probably the greatest athlete of my day. He was a great broad-jumper. He was the finest running halfback in college football. He was a great baseball player. And basketball may have been his best sport.

But what I admired Robinson most for, was that he was a winner. The object in baseball—as it is in any other sport —is to win. But figure-happy baseball frequently forgets this. The player of the year is not always on the winner of the year. The rolls of the sport are barnacled with the names of athletes who quite clearly put individual achievement ahead of team achievement.

Ty Cobb led his team to a pennant when he was a rookie and near-rookie. Then he became Ty Cobb—the super-star of baseball—and he fought his own teammates as enthusiastically as he did the others. Cobb got his hits, batting championships, stolen bases. But the guy playing alongside him he didn't even speak to. That may have had more to do with the fact his teams never again got in a World Series than what Cobb did at the plate.

There are many others of the same persuasion. But not Jack Roosevelt Robinson.

Before he came to them, the Dodgers had won only two pennants in forty-six years. After he got there, they won six pennants in ten years, lost another in a post-season playoff, and still another on the last game of the season. They never finished lower than second. Since he left, they have won one pennant in five years.

Jackie fought his enemies, not his teammates. He never held grudges—except against that persistent foe, Jim Crow, who is in traction and whose throat is rattling today because of the number of times he got in Jackie Robinson's way on the base-paths of life.

Jackie has had to battle since he was old enough to cry. Six months after he was born in a Georgia sharecropper's cabin, his father shoved off for parts unknown with another woman. Jackie's mother, in one of the sagas of courage that should put her in whatever Hall of Fame they have for mothers, took her whole brood across country to Pasadena, a strange city in a strange state where they were about as welcome as the smog.

Jackie got into the kind of scrapes every little kid gets into—swimming in the reservoir, swiping golf balls in the rough at the country club, dumping tar on the lawn of a cranky landlord. Yet he wasn't every little kid. He was colored. But he couldn't go bad because Mallie Robinson wouldn't let him. She hadn't struggled all the way west from a tarpaper cabin to see her children go to an indoor prison instead of a Georgia chain gang.

Jackie got into one famous scrape when he was already a famous football player. The driver of the car he was riding in got into one of those pointless traffic arguments that even the Casper Milquetoasts of society indulge in. Jackie was the peacemaker. But he made peace the way he made everything—aggressively. Before you could say Jack Robinson, he was the one in handcuffs, even though all parties, including the driver of the other car, protested his innocence.

It was a scarlet letter on a police blotter Jackie Robinson could never quite rub off. "Troublemaker!" was the whispered word the bigots hid behind and the well-meaning were troubled by.

But the trouble Jackie made was good for the country like the trouble Lincoln made. In the Army, he refused to play football in protest over a segregated post exchange, he got court-martialled for refusing to sit in the back of the bus. The charge was thrown out.

In baseball, he disagreed with Roy Campanella but didn't retreat into the childishness of not speaking. Jackie always spoke. There was no mistaking where he stood. And it was usually at home plate with the winning run.

He chided the Yankees for discrimination. The Yankees denied it. But went out the next year and got Elston Howard. Some people may not like Jackie Robinson. But they have to respect him. I'm proud he's in the Hall of Fame. But I wish he were also part of the rest of baseball.

Life on the Road

When you're a ballplayer, an off-day is a period of suspended time in which you sit around a hotel lobby and look at a lot of other people who don't have anything to do either.

The trick is to sleep as late as possible because when you wake up you have to think of something to do. And in Philadelphia that's not easy. The last guy to meet the challenge was Sonny Liston and he had to make his own fun. Also his own bail.

The visit of a ball team puts no strain at all on the staffs of art museums and public libraries. And they don't have to double the guards around public monuments. The original manuscript of the Declaration of Independence is as safe from the prying eyes of a baseball player as it was from

King George. Ballplayers read nowadays, but *The Sporting News* still outsells Stendhal.

A ballplayer is in a town but not of it. He wears a path from hotel room to team bus to ballpark and may never stray more than a few feet either way even if he's a twenty-year-man. He can tell you the size, position, botanical characteristics and rate of growth of every potted plant in the lobby. He can tell you every blade of grass in the outfield or infield and exactly how many steps you can take after a foul ball. But he'd have to take a cab to go to Independence Hall if he wanted to go there which he doesn't.

A ballplayer is the only tourist I know of who doesn't take a set of cameras. Andy Carey takes a dressing room shot after every winning game but so far as I know other players only pose for cameras, never shoot one.

He treats the public with impassive reserve, the press with guarded respect. He is at ease only with other ballplayers when he is away from home. An accident of scheduling brought the Houston Colt 45s and the Dodgers here at the same time and the glad fraternization in the lobby of old teammates dropped the guard for a few hours, the Colts outlandish in their blue cowboy suits, high heeled boots and five-gallon hats. But as soon as the Colts' team bus left, the masks dropped again.

They go through lobbies hurriedly, head down, like hunted men. A child cries out, "Look! There's Duke Snider." And they shudder. Recognition means autographs and autographs come with pests attached. "Dook, I seen you hit one offa center-field fence inna Polo Grounds one night, remember?" Duke remembers because a hitter remembers every fence he ever hit anywhere but he doesn't want to discuss it. When a fan corners him for a chat, a ballplayer is polite but he never listens.

He has signed his name oftener than a court clerk but he is well aware that a hastily scrawled "sincerely yours" is no earthly good to the pest with a pen but they just want to be able to reach out and touch their baseball hero and separate themselves from the vast anonymous faceless fandom at least for 10 seconds. In Cincinnati, Maury Wills signed and then testily turned as the fan walked off and demanded, "Aren't you going to ask anyone else?" Far from being proud to be singled out he wanted someone else pestered.

His is a difficult and exacting science. To be able to hit a ball thrown 60 ft. 6 in. at a rate of 95 miles an hour requires concentration and split-second control of reflexes. There are only five hundred people in the world who know what it's like on a day-in, day-out basis to hit major league pitching. There are another thousand waiting impatiently to find out. A king may be a king because his father was, but a ballplayer is a major leaguer only so long as his averages show he is. He never says "hit a home run," he says "jerk one out of here" because he knows that's all you have time to do at a major league plate and the long, lovely sandlot swing would just be a pretty strike.

A ballplayer can never be caught in a bar except after a night game where a curfew is imposed by the state even if he breaks the one imposed by a ball club. Only that night's starting pitcher can stay out beyond 1 o'clock. Toots Shor once said during the wartime curfew, "Anyone who can't get loaded by midnight, ain't trying."

Conversely, any ballplayer who can make it between the time the game is over—usually midnight—and state curfew, usually 2 A.M., is hustling like hell.

He usually tries to go to a bar not frequented by the old man, the manager. With the Dodgers, this is easy: He

doesn't go into any of them. If he ever did it would be looking for a ballplayer, not a drink. The ballplayer today
knows if he goes into too many of them the management
will begin beckoning to one of those thousand waiting at
the gate and suggesting he go do his drinking in Omaha.

When you're on top the pressure is even worse. "They've
got to catch us, haven't they?" argues Leo Durocher with
some logic. But they can catch you if you start dropping
those ground balls, throwing to the wrong base, lunging at
phantom motions of smart pitchers. All of these things are
easy to do when the pressure is on. It's easy to lose your
balance reaching for a pennant.

Besides, the horse in front can clearly hear the hooves of
the field behind him. The league lies in wait for the top
guy. The first sign of blood and they trace it to its source
like a school of hungry sharks.

When you're on the road, life is a vacuum of boredom
punctuated now and then by flashes of sheer fright where
a ball is soaring over your head that you must catch or lose
the game or a pitch goes by and you think, "My God, it's a
curve."

The enemy is time as well as a team. It's hard to win a
major league ball game. Probably no more than a run or two
separates the best team in this league from the worst. It's
even harder when you have to win six out of ten even away
from home. A road game is like a knife fight in a room in
the dark—only it's the other fellow's room.

Schopenhauer once said, "Life is a useless interruption
of an otherwise peaceful non-existence." So is a road trip.
On the other hand, it's also a non-existence.

FIGHT ON FOR OLD $.C.

Gold Line Stand

Football is, in many respects, the most American game of them all.

It used to be played by scholars who, after a hard day in the Chem Lab, felt the need of a little violent exercise to get their sluggish blood going and the smell of the Bunsen burners off their fingers.

Then, one day, it hired a coach. And football has never been the same since. You will never get it back from the coaches without a struggle. For football coaching is an obsessive profession. It is as fascinating as playing chess with real men. The only thing more exhilarating for a human being with a desire to play God is War.

Football teams used to be picked from student bodies. But it was coaches who first discovered that higher education had everything backward. The strength of a civilization—or at least the *sinew* of one—lay in boys who came from a long line of people who worked too hard with their muscles to develop their brains very much.

Your best football player, in short, was a guy who was too busy doing the family chores on the back forty to attend so much as grade school. The coaches' first enemy, then, was the academician. Once you have outwitted him, a man with an IQ several leagues above yours, outwitting a rival coach was child's play.

An ugly word crept in the lexicon of football: "recruitment." It suggested, which is true, that a football team was no longer an extension of a student body, but was as carefully selected as the German General Staff. The only thing a football team had in common with the institution it purported to represent was a common mailing address. Football players showed up on campus only for practice.

The game was economically important to the country. Advertisers poured millions into it, people stormed the box office, old grads neglected their business to scout up 18-in. necks for their dear old alma mater. "Autumnal madness," the late Ted Husing who built a reputation, a fortune, and ultimately a brain tumor on its frenetic activity, used to call it.

In the late 1930s, the elegant Robert Hutchins, president of the University of Chicago, a rather pretentious institution of learning downwind of the stockyards, noisily dropped football. He came in for a good deal of ridicule until one afternoon in a room under the abandoned football field, Dr. Enrico Fermi perfected an atomic reaction. He had unlocked the secrets of energy, sealed the doom of Nagasaki and Hiroshima, introduced the nightmare of fallout to the universe and, perhaps, started the countdown for all of us. It was an impressive feat, a slap in the face of football, which promptly put on its crepe soles and crept away. Mankind put on its crepe souls.

The game periodically retreats into a shroud of penitence called, for want of a better word, "De-emphasis." In some areas, it was called "sanity." A "sanity" code. The very use of the word proclaims there is something insane about football generically. And perhaps there is.

The pathetic attempts of the educators and its own administrators to cope with it suggest the panic of Dr.

Frankenstein trying to find the knobs to control the creature he has loosed on the world.

It is an exciting, vigorous sport for the spectator. For the
participant, it is a tooth-loosener, concussion-causer, limp-
producer. It is a game that needs both a trainer and physi-
cian at all times. Baseball's Fresco Thompson put the
right, bright light on it when he asked a boy torn between
a livelihood in baseball or football, "What do you want,
son, a career or a limp?"

A surprising number of youngsters are willing to settle
for a limp. The economics get better all the time. So does
baseball's, to be sure, but there are times when baseball,
comparatively, seems to be flickering in public esteem.

The professionals in football captured the fickle fancy of
the paying public some time in the mid-1940s. As this is
written, they still have it. There is something sadistically
rewarding about the crack of two behemoth lines, the swift
surge of color of the men running the pass patterns, the loft
of a football in the crisp air, the sudden clutch of fear as
two guys dive for it—*your* guy and the other guy.

It has already had all the ingredients. It has had *its* scandal. It has had its struggle between two leagues. It has
followed baseball relentlessly down its blazed path and appears to have overtaken it.

It has made college football a little less mad—if only
because there is now an economic rainbow at the end of
the limp, the loose tooth, the torn scalp. It has also made
the colleges training camps for another industry. The only
difference is, if Eastman-Kodak wants a chemist, it must
pay his way—or the chemist must pay his way. Colleges
pay football players' ways. Pro football pays nothing for
its raw material which comes to it with ready-made skills
and ready-made notoriety. It is the most felicitous arrange-

ment in the whole fabric of industry. Even steel pays for its raw materials. Colleges refine the football ore at no cost to the ultimate user.

Television dumps $28 million in the laps of the chief beneficiaries of this largesse, the National Football League. It sits there stunned by its good fortune but makes no attempt to share this boon with colleges, consumers or even the Republic. It has only to sell razor blades or new cars to justify itself. This is easy.

This is Football, 1965. Franchises in professional ranks that once sold for streetcar tokens or just for a simple assumption of debts are almost ready to go on the Big Board. Bidding begins at $7,000,000.

The colleges are caught in the same economic spiral. They are in the penny ante division of the game but they dare not drop out, either. The pennies mount up impressively.

Concussions, limps, arm casts and tooth caps will continue to be in ample supply. There is a bull market in bull athletes. Receipts go up as the tonnage goes up—and a pro line today has a gross weight approaching that of a railroad car.

Football has been fought by mothers, educators, legislators, once even The White House (Teddy Roosevelt told them to tame it or toss it) but nothing can top it. Not even the fact that, at Stagg Field in Chicago, the Atomic Era moved in as soon as football cleats moved out.

If I have attempted anything in reporting it, it is to put a block on coaches who would run away with it—and us— if left to their own devices. As a coaches' medium, the abuses of football can be laid at only one doorstep— theirs. But if Presidents, colleges and Electoral College, are powerless to stop it, a mere sportswriter can only hope to slow it down. Like petting in the park, it will be with us for some time to come and even the moralizers can only hope to keep it from getting worse.

The "Heart" of Football

All right, students, time for our semi-annual examination on how well you have digested the lessons of the football season. Ready? Now, remember, give the first answer that comes to your mind.

Question—Two teams that have lost thirteen games between them, couldn't hold Manual Arts High scoreless, and ran up seven points between them last week while their opposition was scoring eighty-three, meet in the season's finale. What do we call it?

Answer—The Big Game.

Q—Old coach Harry Bear has a boy on his squad who plays football with his elbows, leads the conference in cracking ribs and breaking noses, fights tooth decay four ways—with his fists, knees, elbows and helmet. What does the coach say about this homicidal maniac?

A—He says this boy is all heart and he wishes he had eleven like him.

Q—What if he had eleven like him?

A—Football would be outlawed within a year and they would need a boxing license to play that long.

Q—A team that has crushed nine opponents by lopsided scores, has players four-deep—including eleven already drafted by the pros—meets its traditional rival, a team that is quietly de-emphasizing and has a quarterback who flunked his physical for the Boy Scouts. What do the papers say about this one?

A—You throw the book out the window for this one, they say. When these two meet, anything can happen.

Q—Can it?

A—Well, Team A might get in a plane wreck. If it doesn't, Team B will think *it* did.

Q—Old coach Bo Constrictor has stripped the state of able-bodied football players, emptied the pool halls and the cotton fields and suited up every brass-knuckle ruffian he could find out on bail, and he massacres the teams that had to take his leavings in recruitment. What do we say of him?

A—He's a genius. He could be the greatest military leader of our times if he chose the Army as a career.

Q—Could he?

A—Well, if he had the Russian army, he could beat Albania, if that's what you mean. With him, it's not a football game, it's a gang war. If they did the same thing off the field that they do on it, they'd have to declare martial law.

Q—We have a boy who plays despite four broken ribs, a smashed nose, a sprained ankle and a recent appendectomy. What do we say of him?

A—We say he's got "desire." He's also got a hole in his head. He'll have a plate in it, too, before the season's over. What he desires is not to grow old.

Q—A team plays a schedule that includes four opponents who don't have three real football players between them, one has-been school that is trying to drop football, and a school that is coached by a professor of English Lit. What is it known as?

A—The powerhouse of the South. It's No. 1 in all the polls.

Q—A coach takes a boy from a good family who is good to his mother, God-fearing and polite and turns him into a savage in a steel helmet on the football field. What is this known as?

A—Building character.

Q—Is football too rough?

A—No, football isn't. But sadism is. And some coaches don't know the difference.

De-emphasis—'82 Style

The time is 1982.

As we look in on the tree-shaded campus of UCLA, we see a kindly old figure with gray hair, spectacles and a smoking pipe, tacking a notice on one of those trees. This is biology prof, Terwilliger Carnes, who doubles at this time of the year as football coach at the institution.

The notice reads:

ATTENTION ALL STUDENTS. ANYONE DESIROUS OF PLAYING ON THE FOOTBALL SQUAD REPORT TO COACH CARNES' OFFICE AROUND FIVE-ISH FOR OPENING PRACTICE. TEA WILL BE SERVED BUT BRING YOUR OWN COOKIES.

Behind him, a shadowy figure looms up. This is coach Woolly Mammoth, once a most notorious football mentor whose team, "The Purple Puddle," was the most feared in the land. Coach Mammoth disappeared into the Belgian Congo on a recruiting trip 15 years ago and was not heard of again until just recently when he turned up on campus with a fullback on the end of a rope. He found his football team all right, but they kept him treed for ten years, during which Woolly, so to speak, went ape.

He wanted to suit up the fullback he had captured—beg pardon, recruited. But he got in a tug-of-war with the Zoology Department. They insisted his fullback was the Missing Link and his body should be devoted to science, not football.

Coach Mammoth points to the notice on the tree.

"Twig," he says in astonishment. "You can't get a football team that way!"

Terwilliger blows on his cuffs. "Oh, sure you can, old man. That's the way we have been getting them for years now."

Woolly is consternated. "But they'll just be students!" he protests. "First thing you know you'll have 135-lb. tailbacks and they'll be making up their own plays in the huddle!"

Terwilliger seemed amused. "But that's exactly the way we've been doing it. It's wonderful. You'll never know the suspense it adds to the game. Why, we held Princeton to a hundred points in one game last year. Of course, we only scored 110 ourselves. And one of our players only weighed 118."

"Good Lord! Why did you play him?"

"Oh, his Daddy asked us to. Said he felt the boy was getting too bookish and he wanted him to have some physical contact training and he thought football was the safest. We've got about a dozen boys like that. Their parents don't want them to be too sissyish."

Woolly scratches his head. "But you get a football team out of junior colleges or the swamps. And you *invite* only them out to practice. I remember it clearly. You use students only for tutors. Tell me, how much do you pay your students to play?"

"That's the best part of it, Wool, old boy. Nothing. In fact, there was a time, after the crowds fell off, that their Daddies even furnished the uniforms. But when the public learned football was more fun this way than those old 0–0 games between hired football teams, we not only fill the Coliseum, we made enough money last year off Pay-TV to build a new medical school. We ran the pros out of business. Their game couldn't compare to ours for excitement."

"But what about the old 240-pound football players? Have you sent them back to the Ozarks?"

"Heavens, no! They finally had time to read and they were fascinated with it. They found calculus was easier than audibles. On the last of those squads we had, fourteen of the guys switched from phys-ed to pre-med and one of them perfected that cure for the gout you've been reading about. Some of them became cheerleaders."

Coach Mammoth looks as if he's about to have a stroke. "The Rose Bowl! What about the Rose Bowl!" he shrieks.

Professor Carnes looks puzzled for a moment. "Oh that," he says absentmindedly. "Well, we just pick a Coast team, then put an ad in the papers for anybody that wants to come. Sometimes a team wants to come then changes its mind when it finds out there's this better party being given over the holidays. Then we just get someone else. There's usually two or three schools willing to make the sacrifice."

"What about the Big 10 pact!" screams Woolly, his tusks bared.

"The *what!?* Oh. Yes. You mean that old conference back there. Oh, it broke up in 1965. See, they invited this school to the Rose Bowl and its faculty voted against it. Said there was too much emphasis on the Rose Bowl. Then the students went out and rioted and tore up things and hanged effigies and finally refused to go to classes.

"You can see this proved conclusively the professors were right, there *was* too much emphasis on the Rose Bowl. The next year they substituted chess for football."

Coach Mammoth starts off into the night. "Where are you going?" coach Carnes calls after him.

"Back to the Congo," comes the dispirited answer. "I'm going to start a league there. A polo league."

Color Me Purple

If I were running the football game in the Coliseum Saturday, I would slug the thing "For Adults Only." If I were tuning it on television, I would run the kids out of the room first.

The show should really be titled "The Return of the Purple Gang." The videotape is sure to be banned in Britain where they abhor violence on the "telly."

The Purple Gang is really coach Jim Owens' University of Washington Huskies, a crew that would be four-point favorites over The Untouchables. It's a school of piranha fish in football uniforms, a front line so ferocious that some day a ball-carrier is going to disappear into that crowd of maneaters and never come out. The only trace of him will be a loud belch from a linebacker. Only those covered by all-risk insurance should play it.

The Purple Gang did the most to bring West Coast football fans back from their storm shelters and butterfly charts. Until they crumpled the Big Ten power houses two years in a row in the Rose Bowl, Pacific Coast coaches had about decided the only preparation for Pasadena was prayer.

When Owens first rambled up to Seattle from Texas, fresh from the flesh pits presided over by Bear Bryant at Texas A&M, he cast a glance over the talent and promptly covered his eyes. The first thing he did was put half the squad back in street clothes so there'd be room on his practice field for real football players. The previous coaches had been politicians and the squad contained only voters, not victors. Owens disappeared into bear country and began looking for the track of boys the bears would run from.

He put his team on a diet modeled by the curator of the Bronx Zoo. Anyone caught gulping a milk shake was in danger of becoming the first live tackling dummy in the State of Washington's history. Anyone eating between meals had a terrible stomach ache at practice.

For the first time, the school song "Heaven Help the Foes of Washington!" stopped making people laugh and made them shiver. The fastest guy on the field was the other team's trainer. He had to be. Time was frequently of the essence. Ambulance crews put away the cards when Washington played and arranged for police escorts to the nearest emergency rooms.

The coloring book craze took a new wrinkle in Seattle. "I am the Washington Huskies. Color me Purple. These are the opponents. Color them bloody."

Practice sessions at the Washington stadium sounded like a lion farm in a thunder storm. Owens had three teams, the purple, the gold and the "God Help Them." Escaping the scrubs was about as easy as resigning from the Mafia.

Owens' lines usually average only 200 lb. But they all had 18-in. necks and under them all gristle. They ran out on the field like bulls who had been kept underfed and in the dark. Scrimmages were like human cockfights. Owens reasoned that if you knocked everyone down the guy with the ball would go, too.

They also realized that on every good football team there is one player who represents from twenty to thirty-five percent of its effectiveness. Him, they sorted out and separated from the gang. Legally, but enthusiastically. They were like a crew of mechanics who swarmed over the engine of a car, removed the sparkplugs, turned and said, "Okay, wise guy, now let's see you drive it."

It was not a strategy, said Washington, it was a co-incidence. Nonsense, snorted the league, a coincidence doesn't happen every Saturday.

But it was also good for Western football. The chocolate eclair set gradually disappeared from rosters. Big Ten games became breathers, not blastings.

The Purple Gang takes on the USC Trojans Saturday with New Year's roses at stake. The Trojans' Mel Hein, who scouted Washington Saturday, came home to recommend evacuation, or at least keep the women and children off the streets when the Huskies trample by. The home team is reminded of the story of the time in the Huskies' locker room when Owens told his squad, "Take that bus out by the gate," and when he got out there, there was nothing left but the wheels.

USC's coach Johnny McKay has three teams, too. A colleague has suggested they be titled "Faith, Hope and Charity" and they might throw in "Surrender." A better idea would be to put a blockade around their best player, Hal Bedsole, who may be either watching the game from television or his back by the second quarter. He may already have won his first all-American designation in the

Huskies' dressing room in a vote that automatically quali-
fies him as "Least Likely to Succeed" on Saturday.

Love That Woody

So Woody Hayes is not coming to the Rose Bowl. Dad
rat it! Somebody's always spoiling the fun.

It's not that I think Woody Hayes is a great or profound
human being. On the contrary. He's a football coach. Not
the Billy Barnes or Johnny McKay type but the pure article.
The Bear Bryant school. You know. "Winning is the only
thing." That jazz.

Woody always fascinated me. I mean, I have seen guys
who were ungracious losers. But Woody was the most ungracious winner I have ever seen. He always broke me up.
A loud, lovable character who went through life the way
his fullbacks go through a line—knocking people down who
get in his way. Once it was a couple of sports writers.

Woody has a thing about sports writers. He thinks
they're spies. Personally, I've only known about two in my
life who had any idea what they were looking at in a football practice but Woody even suited up his local sports
writers once as though they were war correspondents and
he was General MacArthur.

When he came to the Rose Bowl in 1954–55, Woody
wouldn't let any stranger with a pencil within five hundred
yards of his practice field. He had all the manners of an
invited guest who insists on bringing his own food-taster
to a party.

He slammed USC 20–7—to the surprise of no one—in a

quagmire. After the game, he allowed, in answer to a newsman's question, that his opponents of that day, the Trojans, would be hard put to stay out of the cellar in *his* conference. When pressed, he ticked off six Big 10 teams that could positively beat USC and two that could extend them. Next, he gave the Tournament of Roses committee the back of his hand for allowing bands to march on the field between the halves. People were afraid for a while Woody was going to protest the Rose Parade for disturbing the concentration of his players.

In 1958, he was more subdued—but not much. The Oregon team he was to meet that year was widely believed to be a junior college team with delusions of grandeur. It wasn't. But when Woody came out, he relented somewhat —not to the extent of throwing his practices open to Western writers but to the extent he would personally screen any Ohio State game pictures they wanted to see.

This would have the effect of giving the writer the opportunity to type an excellent story on the Michigan game, for instance, but most sports editors wanted news, not history, and they declined. Even so, Woody got one taker—a scribe who staggered out of the screening and dubbed Ohio State "Murder, Inc."

In the game that followed that year, "Murder, Inc." almost got murdered. Woody's attack is about as unsubtle— and unstoppable—as dinner call at the dog pound. He usually gets the biggest fullback money can buy—speaking figuratively, of course—and hands him the ball and points toward the goal line. Woody has always had a pathological abhorrence of the forward pass, a fact which simplifies the other team's defensive patterns (nine-man line most of the time) but which still doesn't help them.

When Woody barely escaped with a 3-point win in 1958,

he did not relegate Oregon to the Big 10 second division—not exactly—but he took the dressing room podium to bellow: "Quick now! Who was the star of the game?" Reporters who had just voted Oregon's Jack Crabtree star of the game stared open-mouthed. Before anyone had a chance to answer, Woody answered for them. "Don Sutherin!" he yelled, singling out the Buckeye halfback who had kicked the winning field goal but had not played another minute of the game.

Later, when someone mildly suggested Oregon had played a fine game—which they sure had—Woody snorted, "Sure, but they didn't deserve to win. The best team always wins. And we won."

That's old Woody. Our own Fred Flintstone. You can see how we'll all miss him at Pasadena this year.

I can't help chuckling when I read all those brave statements out of Columbus about Woody choking back the tears and pleading for solidarity between cap and gown and helmet and shoulder pads. But I also read where Woody took an hour-and-a-half walk around the hotel just before that, giving himself a good talking-to. I would much rather read *those* quotes.

All the same, I still wish Woody were coming back to Pasadena again this year. It's much worse getting murdered by some Nice Nelly coach who pretends it's hurting him more than you.

Loyal Sons on High

Almost forty years ago, sitting in a drafty press box in the Polo Grounds after a football game, a sportswriter felt a surge of once-in-a-lifetime inspiration. He leaped to his typewriter:

"Outlined against a blue-gray October sky, the Four Horsemen rode again . . ." wrote Grantland Rice. And overnight, a small Catholic university in the northernmost corner of Indiana became a more famous institution of higher learning on the sidewalks of America than Yale, Harvard, or MIT could ever hope to be. But for a lot of the wrong reasons, all of them in shoulder pads.

Rice's kernel harvested into a bumper crop of publicity for the somewhat-surprised good fathers of Notre Dame. There were movies like *The Spirit of Notre Dame, Knute Rockne, All-American,* there were endowments—usually forwarded by cigar-smoking types who inquired eagerly in the next breath what the prospects were for fifty-yard-line season tickets. There was even a motorcar called the "Rockne." There were spirited renditions of "Cheer, Cheer for Old Notre Dame" sung by emotion-choked truck drivers who had never gone beyond the seventh grade. It never occurred to anyone that one went to Notre Dame for an education. In the popular mind, it was a campus populated by halfbacks in hip pads and halfwits in racoon coats.

The formula for synthetic rubber was discovered at Notre Dame but the synthetic alumni couldn't care less. A formula for beating Army was all they wanted. Notre Dame usually provided that, too.

In time, of course, this was to prove an embarrassment to the university. It was like being followed by an over-affectionate litter of Saint Bernard puppies wherever one went. Priests tried to explain the cultural advantages of the university but the audience's heads would begin to nod until the question-and-answer period when someone would ask brightly, "What kind of football team are we going to have this year, Father?"

National intellectual magazines, including some Catholic ones, began to jeer. One ran a photo of Father Sorin with his arms upstretched and the caption sneered "A Fair Catch?" The very dignity of the Church seemed at times at issue.

When Rockne died, a succession of inept coaches alleviated the problem. Then, Francis William Leahy was hired, and even for Notre Dame he put a new dimension on winning. He lost only eleven games in eleven years against competition Rockne never dreamed of. He did it in such a charming way there wasn't a football coach in the country who wouldn't have cheerfully bought him a drink—of arsenic.

He even gave football tryouts—until he got caught at it. He regarded the loss of a game the way most people would regard the loss of an eye. An austere man, his dedication to football was such he once protested the construction of a second story on a classroom because it overlooked the practice field and an opportunity for spying. He could never put the right note of humor on his perfection as Rockne did. Traditional opponents began to drop out like swatted flies and to suggest icily that Notre Dame schedule the Green Bay Packers instead.

There wasn't a dry eye on the sidewalks of New York alumni when Leahy quit, but you could have read your prayers in the light of the candles lit by the faculty. Terence Patrick Brennan was hired and they gave him just enough football players to keep Catawba from trying to get on the schedule but not enough to give Michigan State a real scrimmage. Even the ghost of Granny Rice was in the wings scolding when the good fathers wearily gave up and hired a pro coach to bring Notre Dame back to a semblance of its old prestige.

Outlined against a blue-gray October sky in the Notre Dame backfield this year will be four students. Notre Dame would now rather be known for one scientist than Four Horsemen. The only tryouts football players have to go through are college boards.

Coach Joe Kuharich, who came from ranks where they don't care if a boy can spell if he can catch a football and prove he's not wanted by the police, is a least likely looking candidate for this delicate transition job. Joe looks as rough as a tire iron, but speaks as softly as a new rector. He has quietly accepted academic restrictions critics freely predicted would send him screaming into the streets of South Bend.

Normally, football players are spoiled darlings in their home communities and not at all conditioned to go to a university where they can't have their own cars and their night life is spent sleeping. But Notre Dame, which has turned out a few boys with a limp, tries not to turn one out with one in his morals. Joe is reconciled to the fact the thunder of the Four Horsemen has died to an echo.

"They are building a $13,000,000 library, a radiation lab, and an IBM center at Notre Dame. We are building a football program and we want to do nothing in one that will embarrass the other," Joe says. "You will find that over the past fifteen years, monogram men in Notre Dame football had a 99 percent graduation record." Joe has to keep it that way, with victory if possible, with defeat if necessary. It's hard on the press box poets but easy on the repose of Father Sorin.

What's in a Name?

On my recent swing through the East and Midwest, I chanced upon a picture in a New York paper of a Rome restaurant owner named Remington Olmstead. He was identified in the caption as "former USC halfback."

He isn't. He is a former UCLA halfback, an important difference I am sure you will agree.

But I think I know why they made the mistake. "Remington Olmstead" *sounds* like it belongs in the USC backfield. USC backfields *always* have Remington Olmsteads in them, if you know what I mean.

When I was a kid back in Connecticut I used to love USC backfields. You had to be fascinated. I remember rolling the names off my tongue. Morley Drury. Homer Griffith. Grenville Landsdell. Gaius Shaver. Irvine Warburton. Orville Mohler. You read them and felt like going out and throwing rocks at your mother and father for naming you "Jim" when they could have picked something romantic and sturdy like these lucky guys.

There was Ambrose Schindler. Aramis Dandoy. There was my all-time favorite. Name, not player. "Ellsworth Kissinger." You had to sneer when you thought of other teams with a lot of guys named "Mike" or "Butch" or "Pug" on them. The USC team sounded as if it had been made up by Sir Walter Scott. Take Marshall Duffeld, for example. You hear that name and your first guess is he's the lead in *Ivanhoe.*

The best part about these guys is they were all good, too. I recall my uncles who were great football fans telling me that no one could really beat the Trojans because they grew kids two inches taller and twenty pounds heavier in California. They were all Olympic sprinters. They all had blond hair and swam to Catalina before breakfast every morning.

It makes me kind of sad when I think about it. Nowadays, they tell me the kids are tougher back East because they are brought up in coal mines and have snow and ice to battle and drink real water, not piped in mirages. It's the fault of that damned Rose Bowl.

I bring all this up because I wandered out to the USC practice field the other day to get a look at the new Trojans who open the season Friday. You know who's going to be the great player of this era? Willie Brown.

Now, I know a rose by any other name runs as sweet and, believe me, Willie with a football in his hands will do much to restore the old legend about kids raised in California. But you can't help feeling sad that mothers don't read *The Lives of the Poets,* or Virgil, or *The Lady in the Lake* any more. I mean, what has happened to the Addison Hawthornes? Hillard Hills?

What has happened to the ringing strophes of yore? Garrett Arbelbide. Courtney Decius. Logan Wheatley. Elwyn Caley. Those were players whose names were as graceful as they were, and made you wish your own name was Cholmondely (pronounced Chumley). Ah, for Orlando Ferrante! Volney Peters! These, I submit, are the stuff that made USC great.

"The Thundering Herd" was a local nickname picked by writers who had heard the earth tremble when the Trojans ran out of the tunnel. The rest of us leaned to Plutarch's *Lives* for nicknames. Desmond Koch! A blond bull who could kick a football or hurl a discus out of sight.

The Herd hasn't thundered much in recent years. The floor of the Coliseum still trembles but the opposition doesn't. "The Blundering Herd," is the new nickname favored by disillusioned writers.

It's a new era. Coach Johnny McKay faces Georgia Tech Friday night with the lightest USC team in years. No more can rival coaches alibi their own shortcomings by saying "the Trojans have all the material." USC is as hard to get into as Yale, even for a football player, maybe especially for a football player. President Norman Topping went shopping for foundation money which every private institution needs in this day of the state-subsidized octopus and was told USC's academic image came into focus wearing a sweat shirt and a shoulder pad.

Dr. Topping has now remolded that academic image and it is held in deep respect, its faculty saluted by national magazines.

But it's the football team I'm worried about. I sincerely think for USC that is an important part of its image.

Johnny McKay faces a typically skilled and fast Bobby Dodd team from Georgia Tech, a squad which has been in more Bowls than Campbell's Soup of late. I hope Johnny gets football players like Garrett Arbelbide or Orville Mohler. Even if their names are "Jack" or "Joe" or even real dull like "Jim Murray." And I wish John would change his name to "Gardner." Just for old time's sake.

Splendid Spectator

George Ratterman, the eminent law enforcement officer from Kentucky, is a guy who will never make the pro football Hall of Fame. But he should.

George told why in an issue of *The Saturday Evening Post*. George played football for fourteen years. As a pro, he racked up $172,965 without ever getting racked up himself. He doesn't say how much he made as a collegian, but George managed all this money without ever being carried off the field in a stretcher.

In fact, the way he tells it, that would have been the only way they ever could have got him out on the field. George was as adept as a New York waiter in avoiding the eye of the coach—particularly when the situation was grave. *How to Succeed in Football without Really Playing* should be the title of his autobiography, Ratterman suggests, instead of what it is, *Confessions of a Gypsy Quarterback*.

George's concentration on NOT playing was so persevering that once when regular quarterback Otto Graham was knocked cold and out in a Cleveland Browns-49er game in 1953, Ratterman leaned over and asked coach Paul Brown, "Do you want me to go in or should we forfeit the game?"

History doesn't record Brown's answer, but Graham was back in the game for the second half even though his face had so many stitches it looked like a wall motto. Ratterman's attitude indicated to Brown he better get Graham in there if he had to put him in an iron lung between plays.

On another occasion, when Ratterman couldn't avoid

playing a full game, he found, to his horror, he was winning it, 62–14. But he was equal to the occasion. He invented a hokey story about how the victims, the Giants, were so wracked by dissension they hadn't even tried to play. It was the closest call of Ratterman's career. He almost became a first stringer that afternoon. If the coaches knew the Giants were leveling, success might have spoiled George Ratterman.

"Ratterman," a teammate once complained, "you don't use a whole roll of adhesive tape all season." They called baseball's Ted Williams "The Splendid Splinter" because of his performance afield. They called George Ratterman that because he looked like he came with the bench. His only casualties in ten years of pro ball were slivers. "I retired with a full quota of arms and legs," he boasts. His nickname should have been "The Splendid Spectator."

It was a battle of wits between him and his coaches and some of them, he says, were only half armed. "Way down deep inside their thick furry bodies," he says, "coaches are sometimes good men, kind and devoted to their families—except possibly during the season."

He quotes George Halas as picking an eager young rookie off the bench once late in a tight game and instructing him, "Taylor, we've run out of time-outs. Go in and get hurt."

Says Ratterman: "Outsiders may wonder if coaches are people. To me, the question seems absurd. Of course they aren't."

The mayhem is so major that one time a coach was chewing out a player because a rival end was out-thinking him. "Don't worry, coach," the player, who weighed 230 pounds, soothed. "After I hit him a few more times, he'll be as stupid as I am."

Ratterman is now high sheriff of Newport, Kentucky, a

gambling town just across the river from Cincinnati where he won the election after some hair-raising goings-on in the midst of which Ratterman, otherwise known in football as "The Kid," was found in a hotel room with what mightly loosely be described as no lady but not his wife either. George proved it was a frame-up.

Reminds me of the time the Irish politician in Boston was similarly framed and he staggered back to precinct headquarters with a harrowing tale of how his political enemies had bound him and kidnaped him and put him in a room where they poured whiskey down his throat for four days. "Couldn't you have escaped before now?" he was asked. "Oh, sure," he said. "But Oi was having too good a toime."

What puzzles me is, now that George is sheriff, who is he going to get to make the arrests?

Ifs, Ands, and Butts

The best lie detector I know has big brown eyes, a nice shape, hair that changes color every so often, and makes lousy coffee.

I had to marry her to find out she was a walking polygraph machine. She doesn't need any electrodes. Your blood pressure and pulse have nothing to do with it. She just looks into your eyes for a minute or two and says "you're lying." And, by golly, you are.

Criminology lost a great aid the day I put her in the kitchen and my life became unbelievably complicated. I didn't stop lying altogether, just around the house.

I bring this up because I'm thinking of volunteering her services to the sovereign states of Alabama and Georgia to settle a border dispute. At issue is not a boundary but a football game. It's the biggest topic of conversation in the South since secession and may have almost as far-reaching effects.

You're familiar with the broad outlines: a couple of character builders of national repute, coach Bear Bryant of Alabama and athletic director Wally Butts of Georgia, stand accused of taking some of the suspense out of the Georgia-Alabama game last year. Their accuser is a kind of improbable character who can vouch for the fact that if you listen in on other peoples' phone conversations you hear the darnedest things.

There's a federal rap against it but if enforced they'll have to throw half the rural housewives in the Middle West behind bars. Besides, it's all right to report a capital offense if you overhear one in the making and if fixing it for Georgia to lose to Alabama isn't high treason, the country is really going soft.

The accuser is George P. Burnett, who sells insurance (and phone conversations) for a living. He wouldn't be able to sell a life policy in an air raid in Alabama the way things now stand. And both Butts and Bryant have fired off lawsuits in amounts high enough to restore the Confederacy against the Yankee magazine that printed Burnett's charges.

This is where my wife comes in. In the immortal words of Boston Blackie, someone is lying here. Someone usually is. There are those who think it's Butts and Bryant. Football coaches have had a great deal more experience at it than the general run of the public. On the other hand, insurance salesmen are not exactly above reproach, as you will find out if you read the fine print some time. And Burnett turned out to have written a few checks in his time that were full of lies.

In a situation like this, the authorities have no choice but to call on science which, in its madness, has perfected machines which cannot quite tell when you are lying but can tell when you are not telling the truth. This is not always, but usually, the same thing.

The trick in these machines is the question. You all know, I am sure, how a man feels when he is lying. He blushes a little, his pulse gets rapid, his blood pressure soars and his teeth ache a little. It's the suspense, you understand. He's hoping you believe him.

My wife can notice all these things instantly from across the room but cops are not so gifted. And courts of law often don't want to find out the truth because it's such a bother.

Burnett took his lie detector test and he either passed it or he's got low blood pressure. Butts, who cries a lot, invoked the Almighty, Jefferson Davis and the infield fly rule. But he showed a great respect for the lie detector machine, maybe on the theory they would ask him if it was true Charley Trippi just walked on campus one day and asked if he could try out for the team.

Bear Bryant, as usual, had a trick play. He just ambled down and took his own lie detector test. Bear, also as usual, was a 35-point favorite going into it and it was announced he had passed. The decision, presumably, was unanimous. It was the neatest trick since Big Julie threw the dice in a hat in *Guys and Dolls* and announced he had won. Nathan Detroit took his word for it but to this day he doesn't know what Big Julie's point was. The dice had no pips on them, you see.

The outcome was enormously encouraging to Butts who dried his eyes and went down to Jacksonville where an ex-sportswriter named Joe Livingston had a lie-spotter all of his own. I mean, no home should be without one.

This machine scorned the elaborate equipment those big city slickers use. It had two little clips you fasten on your thumbs which is a part of the anatomy that flinches first when you go to lying as any fool can plainly see. Butts came out of it like George Washington.

Of course, since none of this is admissible in any court except possibly that one in *Alice in Wonderland,* no one can ever, so to speak, call Butts a liar. And you can't cross-examine a man's thumbs anyway. He told the truth seventeen straight times, his interrogator said, which is a pretty good average even if he only asked him about the weather. I mean, I don't believe I know seventeen direct items of fact in a row. I have to hedge right after giving my name, rank and serial number.

It's encouraging, though, when lie detector machines begin to fall out among each other. There's a faint ray of hope for mankind yet. To outwit a machine, even one that only has you by the thumbs, is a slap in the teeth for automation and I'm all for it. Bill Castell, of the Jacksonville paper, one whom I spoke to on this curious affair, is in complete accord. "I'm a rubber hose man myself," he announced unequivocally.

So, I have to think, am I. There are times when the good old Third Degree is the last hope of mankind and this may be one of them.

But I am also vastly buoyed to know that you can now buy a lie detector machine of one's very own—$169 F.O.B. Michigan City, Ind. I hope to get the exclusive West Coast distributorship because I think it's just the ticket for the man who has everything, particularly a blonde on the side.

An all-purpose lie detector is just the thing for around the house when you don't want to face that old-fashioned lie detector—a wife. And when you say "honest, honey, we were just talking business," the machine says "that's right" instead of "tilt." We'll market the machine under the name of its discoverer's autobiography—"no ifs, and—or Butts."

Honesty Is the Policy

Norman Van Brocklin, man and boy, quarterback and coach, has always been a guy with the nice even disposition of a top sergeant whose shoes are too tight.

He is one of the most painfully honest interviewees in the world of sport where, to be sure, the contention doesn't run deep. But Norm is the only guy I know who couldn't be trusted to say something nice at the funeral about Albert Schweitzer.

It's not just that Dutch doesn't like the Los Angeles press—or the Philadelphia press either, for that matter. This doesn't make a man all bad.

It's just that Dutch thinks everybody is out to red-dog him and he doesn't want ever to be caught on the blind side. Throughout his career, Norm felt he was the victim of myopic owners, lead-footed ends who dropped passes they should have caught with boxing gloves, fullbacks who pretended to slip when they had to block Gino Marchetti, and halfbacks who missed audibles and left Van Brocklin standing there holding out a football and feeling foolish because there was nobody there to take it but Marchetti.

On top of this, there was Les Richter whom Dutch didn't like because of the way he combed his hair, and Sid Gillman whose trouble was he was the coach. Van Brocklin is one of the few employees in industry who went to the owners and suggested they get rid of either him or the boss— and then was surprised when it was him.

In a way, you can't blame Dutch Van Brocklin. One of the greatest quarterbacks in the annals of football, a sure first-draft choice in the Hall of Fame, he had to go through the indignity of sharing his job throughout most of his career. The analogy is to imagine Babe Ruth being platooned.

The platooning made sense when Dutch's alternate was Bob Waterfield. Dutch will be lucky to make the Hall of Fame in a dead heat with Waterfield. But when it was Billy Wade who benched Dutch Van Brocklin from time to time, Dutch kept looking over to see if the coach had the decency to blush. The other teams in the league wouldn't believe their luck and held their sides laughing at such times. With Wade in there, the 40-yard line was a goal line stand for the Rams—even when they had the ball.

When he moved on to Philadelphia, Dutch led the Eagles to their first championship in eleven years and was glowingly promised the head-coaching job. "You will live to see your grandchildren go to school in Philadelphia," they promised him—a prospect which would send a chill down my spine but which sounded fine to Van Brocklin.

Instead, of course, he didn't even stick around long enough to see his children enroll for the fall term. The owners wanted Van Brocklin in uniform, not in the front office.

Small wonder Van Brocklin has come to expect the worst

of football. When he was offered the Minnesota Vikings job, he waited around to see what the catch was. Pretty soon, he saw it: the Minnesota Vikings. A collection of guys interrupted on their way to a rocking chair after a long, liniment-scented career of head-knocking in the NFL or a bunch of bushy-tailed youngsters who would think they had fallen down an elevator shaft the first time Joe Schmidt up-ended them. They looked more like an office picnic than a football squad.

Van Brocklin, as always, went to the heart of the matter. "A bunch of stiffs," he characterized his team in a fit of candor that gave them all the morale boost of an intercepted pass.

Van's "bunch of stiffs" took on the Rams here Sunday in a game that was even hard for the coaches to stay awake through. Van's team made more mistakes than a boss the first time his secretary runs her fingers through his hair. And it was a good thing. Because the Rams were in the hunt with them for the lead in mistakes. Both teams displayed what Charlie Maher would describe as "mid-season formlessness."

Metropolitan Stadium, where the game was played, is a curious structure strategically located between Minneapolis and St. Paul so neither will be offended. The architecture, I would say, is early Erector Set. It may not be a bad place to watch a baseball game but for football, the La Brea Tar Pits would serve as well.

The score of the game was 21–17 and to give you an idea, the winning touchdown was scored by that offensive scourge, Les Richter. When you get beat by a 42-yd. broken-field run by Les Richter, you have a right to make the air blue and I fully expected the sulphur content to be above health limits before I even got close to Van Brocklin.

But Dutch was as placid as a winner. I still got the illustrated lecture about the role of journalism in sports (to
Dutch, as parasitical as moss on a strong tree) but he was
smiling when he said it. In such cases Dutch is like a dog
barking and wagging his tail. You're never sure which end
to believe.

"I was happy the way we played the second half. When
you come back from 21–3 to lose by 4 points you can be
happy. I know now I have two real good football players,
Tommy Mason and Fran Tarkenton. I think Tarkenton
did the right thing in unloading the ball even after shaking
off the rush. He has 15 years ahead of him in this league
and I don't want him getting hurt at the start."

In the other dressing room, his old running mate, Bob
Waterfield, was not about to split playing time in the papers
with Dutch, too. A man whose honesty is less explosive but
no less resolute than Van Brocklin's, Waterfield observed.

"We could have scored many more points—maybe 40 if
we left Zeke Bratkowski in there. But we're trying to get
ready for a league season, not run up exhibition scores.
Dutch has done a good job with that team but his quarterback, Tarkenton, can't go scrambling around there out of
the pocket like he did and win many games and Dutch
knows it."

If he doesn't, of course, we can expect Minnesota fans
to begin to chant "We Want Wade" any day now.

Hall of Infamy

I won't say it's hot in Redlands—but have you ever seen birds sweat?

The Rams hold their training camp here so the least exertion will boil the fat off their athletes. I know. I lost 4 lbs. just getting out of bed in the morning. I don't know how that circus fat lady dropped 400 pounds in a year but I know she could have done it a lot sooner in Redlands.

Actually, the natives consider the present weather quite cool. It was a nippy ninety-five the day I got here. Any cooler and the locals go around in ear muffs.

I did not come down here entirely to scout the Rams. It's too early yet to tell much about them. You see, even the rookies haven't been given their bus tickets home yet. You know the ones I mean—the phenoms who beat Ollie Matson in wind sprints and get in fist fights with each other when the coaches are looking to show they got spirit. Not talent, just spirit.

The coaches keep them around just so the regulars will get used to crowds but the rookies don't catch on. They actually think the Rams will put Jon Arnett on waivers to make room for them.

I really came down to Redlands as a scout for my friend, Len Pucci, the Valley restaurateur, who is involved in the program to establish a National Football League Hall of Fame in his old hometown of Canton, Ohio. He's looking for suggestions for candidates and I think I can come up with a few.

I will go right by the obvious first choices—men like

Sammy Baugh, Don Hutson, Bob Waterfield. I am thinking more of the men who might be overlooked in the early balloting but men who have meant much to the game. For instance:

Bobby Layne—Bobby's glass case should contain a large pile of olives and toothpicks representing the all-time record for the most completions of martinis.

Jon Arnett—Jon's jersey will be retired with Big Daddy Lipscomb's draped over it so people will recognize it quicker.

Jim David—Jim's trophy room will include a pile of crutches including the ones he put Tom Fears on, the jaw splint he put Y. A. Tittle in and the dustpan full of loose teeth, including some of his own, they always swept up in Jim's defense zone after a game.

Pat Harder—Harder's memorial will be the helmet with which he broke Lenny Ford's jaw. Ford's original teeth and pieces of jawbone will be sticking out the top.

Dan Reeves—Dan will be represented in the "love thy neighbor" exhibit in company with the other Ram owners. They will be shown having each other for dinner. That is to say, the exhibit will actually depict Reeves buttering Ed Pauley up. Or putting ketchup on Fred Levy.

Gino Marchetti—Marchetti will be shown in full uniform—wearing Billy Wade as a watch fob. Or under his arm like a brief case.

Billy Wade—Billy will make it as the game's biggest eater —of footballs. Wade will be shown bumping into a door and dropping the football on the way out of the dressing room. He will also be honored as the only man in the game ever to lose ten yards to a tackling dummy.

Otto Graham—Otto will be singled out as the all-time holder of the record for mouth stitches. His will be a sculpture with an anonymous hand sticking out of his mouth. It will be in the sportsmanship room under a scroll by Pete Rozelle on the inspiration pro football has been to youth and youth organizations—like the cub Mafias.

George Strugar—George will be the only lineman honored for most forward passes attempted—on airline stewardesses. Also for the all-time reception of face slaps in a single season.

Ed Sprinkle—Sprinkle will be honored as the man who set the record for nosebleeds in opposing quarterbacks and the man who did the most to make the Wrigley Field first-aid crew the most experienced in football.

George Halas—Halas will be placed in the good sport room in recognition of his outstanding contributions to ending signal-stealing and referee-baiting. Also for refusing to sell season tickets on the Ram bench to good customers. Special note will be taken of the time he refrained from knocking down the grandmother he was taking a ball away from in the stands.

Paul Brown—Will win the all-heart award as the coach who has done the most to encourage self-reliance in quarterbacks. Bronze plaque will show Paul on the two-way radio to his signal caller who is also shackled to Brown's leg on a short chain. Caption should read: "Play it any way you want, son. It's just a game."

There will be a special room for linebackers like Don Paul and Joe Schmidt. They will be shown drinking blood.

THE SWEET SCIENCE

Dillinger Died Here

Chicago again. That toddling town. State Street, that not-so-great street. George Washington never slept here but John Dillinger died here.

I came back for the fight—Patterson vs. Liston. St. George and the Dragon.

Actually I came to protect my interests as a journalist. A "journalist" was identified by a member of the British press on hand here as "a gentleman who borrows money from a newspaperman."

Anyway, all the heavyweights of journalism are here— Jim Braddock, Joe Louis, Archie Moore, Jack Dempsey— men whom some editors consider the ablest historians of our day. The minute a plane puts down and Art Aragon or Hurricane Jackson steps out of it carrying a pencil and typewriter I know I'm entering the twilight zone. So is the business.

The function of these gentlemen is to plot the fight for you and pick the winner. They delay picking the winner as long as possible. Till after the fight, if possible. Their record is so bad, even then they'd be wrong. They have an unwritten code (an unwritten code is a code in the head) with the promoter that if one picks one fighter, the other will pick the other. That way they'll not only sell tickets but be 50 percent correct. They all carry their own ghost writers with them—so called because they never write until after midnight. They're too sober before that.

I have found a way to hold off this army of invisible competition. I don't carry a ghost writer with me; I have a ghost fighter. Studs Conway, the duration heavyweight champion of the minesweeper Corvette K-38, U. S. Navy.

Studs had more one-round knockouts on his record than any other fighter in history. He even won one of them.

Studs, our mythical ghost fighter, is going to analyze the mythical championship bout between Cloudy Piston and Loyd Mattersone for us as we approach him in his hotel room, pencil in hand.

Question—Studs, how do you size up the fight for our four million readers?

Answer—I see it as gavotte. It should be staged in the Aragon Ballroom, or the Lawrence Welk Show.

Q.—Who will win it?

A.—I can't see how either of them can. If the referee bumps into either one, he should be the favorite.

Q.—How do you think you'd do against either of them?

A.—To tell the t'root, I could knock them out by phone. The champ'd go down if you hit him with a Kleenex and Cloudy is so slow he couldn't get out of the way of a glacier.

Q.—What kind of a fight will the champ make?

A.—Cautious. I expect him to get a Boy Scout to help him across the ring.

Q.—What was the toughest fight you ever had?

A.—My first wife.

Q.—She was good and game?

A.—Game! I hit her with the best left hook I ever threw and she didn't even blink. She had the sneakiest right in the business. She'd wait till you were asleep before she threw it. We didn't get a divorce. They awarded her a TKO.

Q.—I understand you've taught the challenger a few things.

A.—Yeah. I taught him to eat with a knife and fork and how to write his name and wear shoes.

Q.—He has an amazing record.

A.—Yeah, but he done his time. Nobody's perfect.

Q.—No, I mean his ring record. All those knockouts.

A.—Yeah, but you have to remember the cops were going for their guns at the time and they were set up for the right hand.

Q.—Who is the superior ring general?

A.—They're both privates.

Q.—Do you care to make a prediction, champ?

A.—The fight will be over with the first punch. But if the champ trips going into the ring they could count a hundred over him and he won't get up. But the other guy's so slow it will take him two rounds to get off his stool. He won't get to the center of the ring for the introductions till the fifth round. The ref will think he didn't show up. If they have a 24-foot ring they'll be so far apart they won't even recognize each other if they meet on the street the next day.

Q.—What do you think the crowd'll be?

A.—Asleep.

Q.—Well, thanks, champ, I got to rush this on the wire now. See you at the fight.

A.—Not me. I'm going to the Roller Derby that night. If you want to see real fights, forget them clumsy Palookas. Give me the broads. They'd scare Hitler.

I had my story. And I flashed it back to my editor on the Pismo Beach *Daily Equivocator:*

Ex-champ sees savage battle.

Champ's ring generalship will tell.

Spine-tingling battle expected. "Wouldn't miss this one if I had to cross the street for it," states Conway.

High and Low Life

Edward Michael Walker, the fist fighter, will best be remembered as the middleweight who had the best left hook and the biggest thirst in the business. If it hadn't been for the one, the thirst, the other, the hook, might have made him the only 150-pound heavyweight champion in modern history.

When he wasn't fighting the bottle, Mickey Walker was usually fighting heavyweights. The only difference was he could hold his own with the heavyweights. He found them so easy to hit and beat, he even fought them dead-drunk on occasion to even the odds a bit.

One such was the eve of the 1930 Kentucky Derby when the pocket-sized Walker climbed in with a 220-pound, 6 foot 3 inch brute named Paul Swiderski. You have heard of fighters staggering out of the ring. Mickey staggered into it. Anywhere else, and his police escort would have arrested him as a common drunk.

Actually, Mickey was an uncommon drunk. He hit the floor so often in the first round, the referee never bothered to come out of a kneeling position—he knew Mickey would be right back—and Mickey's manager, the foremost ring larcenist of all time, Doc Kearns, reached over and rang the bell with a water bottle while there was still half-a-minute to go in the round.

Doc's reward was a punch in the jaw from Mickey because in his condition he couldn't tell friend from foe. Doc recovered in time to pull a fuse and plunge the arena in darkness the next time Mickey hit the floor. A riot was incited, police were called, and when order had been restored, Mickey was sober and Swiderski was sunk.

This is only one of the riotous instances recalled in Mickey's new biography *The Toy Bulldog & His Times* which I have just finished reading. Mickey had 141 fights in his 100-proof life. He was married seven times, once squandered almost half-a-million dollars on one trip to Paris, got thrown out of hotels for brawling in half the major cities of the world.

Between fights, he leaped into a bottle and pulled the cork in after him. Once, in Hollywood, he bought half of Laurel Canyon from screen star Lloyd Hamilton for $55,000 when both were in their cups. When he sobered up, Mickey unloaded it in panic for $58,000—or about $7,000,000 less than it was worth.

He palled around with Charlie Chaplin, Douglas Fairbanks, Texas Guinan, and Al Capone. He once ran across a ballroom floor to take a punch at the then Prince of Wales. He actually cocked his fist at Capone once when a friend stepped in. "You saved his puss," grumbled Mickey. "I saved your life," the friend corrected.

He was a front-man for a bootlegger, yet he spent half-a-million dollars trying to learn polo and crack society. When he didn't make it, he went on a drunk with a two-bit flunky of a crooked mayor. He was the middleweight champion of the world and a leading contender for the heavyweight title at the time but was stopping gutters like a Bowery bum.

He married and remarried his ex-wives so confusingly that his friends suggested he print up programs with names and numbers of all the players. He dated Norma Talmadge, Lilyan Tashman, Lupe Velez, and once flew all night from Cleveland to New Jersey in a two-seat, two-wing plane with a pilot who shared a quart of Scotch with him. He beat up the whole Notre Dame football team one night just after the Army football team had spent the afternoon unsuccessfully trying to do the same thing.

He lost the most important fight of his career, to Max Schmeling in 1932, because he trained on the golf course —not on golf, on champagne. The caddy carried the bottles. Mickey carried the clubs. No one kept score but on his worst holes Mickey used up three bottles.

Many good fighters take good care of themselves while they are fighting, and take to drink when they're through. Mickey, who often held his victory parties before the fight, reversed the trend here too. One day in 1939, while the radio crackled the news of the start of World War II, Mickey found himself on a bat with a cast of characters he shouldn't even have been talking to. He hoisted a glass of beer and announced, "Gentlemen, this is my last drink. I'll never take another as long as I live."

He never has. Mickey filled the void in his life with painting, a notion that came to him while watching a movie on the life of Gauguin one day. Although some unkind critics suggested he should have taken the boxing gloves off first, his art has been exhibited widely. "It is the only thing," cracked Doc Kearns, "that could keep Mickey Walker on canvas."

His fight friends are even more impressed. "Could Picasso get off the floor fourteen times against Swiderski?" is what they ask.

End of the Champ

At the age of seventeen, Ignacio (Keeny) Teran was, in the critical eyes of the gnarled old mentors of the Main Street Gym, easily the greatest bantamweight prize-fighting prospect since the days of Mexican Joe Rivers.

He was fast. He could hit sharply. He could crumple opponents with a picture-book right cross, a big punch that few bantamweights ever have.

And it was funny because Keeny looked more like a ten-year-old choirboy than a pug. He was almost pretty. Bright brown eyes, even white teeth, a dazzling smile.

As he laughed his way through his first seventeen fights without losing a round and knocking out ten, the boys around the gym began to breathe hard. The bantam division, always talent poor in a country that ate well, was the easiest to crack in pugilism. "Boy," drooled the fight mob admiringly, "a bantam that hits like a heavy!"

Then, something strange happened. In his first main event, the promoters thoughtfully picked a man Keeny had twice beaten, a tough Nisei ex-Army sergeant from Honolulu, Tommy Umeda. It was to be more of a testimonial than a test for Keeny, ten rounds of Ole's! for the next champion of the world.

Only, Keeny never got to go ten. His timing shockingly shoddy, his once-blistering right wreaking as little damage as a dust-cloth, Keeny was knocked out bleeding and dazed in the eighth round.

The display was so bad the fight mob probed to find out why. The trail was easy to follow. It had been well blazed by a number of great Mexican-American prospects before him. The shame, for once, was not boxing's. It was the community's. Keeny was on dope. H. Horse. Keeny had a big habit. He wasn't the coming bantamweight champion of the world. He was a coming derelict. Keeny Teran, the former human being. A society that would call out the National Guard if an army of rattlesnakes appeared on the streets of downtown L.A. was letting an army of pushers go by with a shrug.

It wasn't only Keeny's life by now. He had a pretty little daughter. Boxing promoter Babe McCoy sent him to Texas to a cure. But Keeny didn't want a cure. He wanted a fix. He skipped to L.A., where there was a reporter waiting in his living room for him, Lou Larkin, a typical guy with a notebook and a deadline. Hardboiled on the outside, sentimental as an embroidery on the inside. "Why don't you quit, Keeny?" he asked. Keeny was bitter. "You don't know about heroin, do you? I don't sleep at night. My whole body is screaming for the stuff. By morning, I'm nearly crazy. I try to eat breakfast but I can't touch it. The day goes by like agony."

Larkin spread Keeny's story on page one. The city was instantly sympathetic. The rehabilitation of Keeny Teran became everybody's business. The newspaper whisked him out of town, put him in training. For a "comeback" at the age of nineteen.

The "comeback" was a charade. Keeny was rematched with Umeda in a theatrically staged main event that was equal parts bathos and pathos. Umeda smashed Keeny to the canvas in the sixth round but Keeny staggered to his feet, weathered the round and won the fight. The decision was unanimous; Teran had come back.

Or nearly unanimous. Coming out of the fight, a reporter

bumped into a narcotics cop. He was shaking his head. "You still don't understand the nature of the enemy," he said sadly. "Once you're hooked on 'H,' there's no way out."

It was not the kind of talk the happy-ending hopers wanted to hear. But it was the kind they should have listened to. Keeny Teran could lie to boxing commissions but a Nalline test doesn't listen.

Sequels never make page one. Particularly if they're downbeat.

Keeny Teran tried to kill himself last week. As usual, he bungled the job. Keeny hasn't done anything right since the day he took his first pop of heroin just to go to the beach. "Just to go to the beach I took it," he once wept savagely to me in a Sunset Blvd. restaurant. "Can you imagine such a thing? Just so some big guys would take me with them to the beach! How do you like that for a reason for wrecking your life?"

He put his head on his arms and cried then. I would, too, if I were on my way where he was—prison and worse. I remember thinking, "For that, his mother cleaned out railroad cars all her life." Keeny raised his tear-stained face. "Just think," he almost whispered. "I could of been the bantamweight champion of the whole world!"

The Death of Davey Moore

Can boxing long survive the death of Davey Moore? Should it?

Does a "sport" which has been on parole deserve a full

pardon when it proves again and again it hasn't changed? Do we swallow our conscience one more time and continue to ban bullfights and cockfights while continuing to sanction prize fights? Are animals more precious than human beings? Are duels at dawn more immoral than death in the evening? Do we sell tickets to an execution? Is this the twentieth century or the Roman Empire? How many deaths and comas are over the legal limit?

The evening at Dodger Stadium Thursday featured one fighter who had killed a man in the ring and, as it turned out, another who was about to be killed. It also featured a boy who has been knocked kicking four times in a career so brief he's only been able to vote for a year. Battling Torres had the bad luck to be a drawing card so he got knocked kicking again from a punch so light that his vanquisher fainted dead away. Several of us watching didn't feel too good either.

Whatever he went down from, Battling Torres didn't get up. For that, they can light candles in Reynosa, Mexico, today. He will, thank God, join his family instead of Davey Moore.

Moore's tragedy is he was a good, game fighter. He not only got up, he would still be fighting if his manager hadn't quit for him. It may have been the greatest service Willie Ketchum ever performed for Davey Moore. Davey had taken a savage beating, but he had dealt one out, too. His face was cruelly marked, he had swallowed and shed blood, his step was a stagger and the hysterical sounds of the blood-thirsty crowds in the upper tiers must have sounded nightmarish to his puddled brain as they led him dazed and daunted from the ring. This was the face of boxing up close. We didn't know it, then, but if we had listened we could have heard the raucous, mocking laughter of Death in the background. He didn't know it then but Davey Moore was in a bigger fight out of the ring than he had been in it.

We reporters were milling around his locker room when they led this poor, broken, jockey-sized athlete into the airless little room that serves in a happier sport as manager Walt Alston's summer cubicle. The door was quickly barred. There were yelps of dismay from us gentlemen of the press. We had a deadline, we complained.

So did Davey Moore.

We are important to this spectacle of man's inhumanity to man. So they let us in anyway.

Davey sat up on the dressing table with effort, as if he just heard in the recesses of his hemorrhaging mind his own private referee toll the count of eight. Davey never would take a count.

"It just wasn't my night. I just can't take nothing away from that boy but—" He halted, looked around and tried to focus on the sea of faces around him. "Well," he began pathetically, "you fellows have times when you can't write as well as others." He was right. And this is one of them.

"I know I can fight much better than I did tonight," he almost whispered. His manager demonstrated a severed mouthpiece which had been ripped from his fighter's teeth by a savage right-hand punch. "I offered a doctor a hundred dollars yesterday to make him a new mouthpiece but there wasn't time," he explained.

But it was not Davey's mouth which needed protection. It was his brain. It was bleeding slowly as he talked. It was to gush later but three of us who leaned over to shake his hand as we left the room didn't know that. "I'm awfully glad you stopped it," I told Ketchum.

Apparently, as soon as we left the room, the slow leak became a burst.

An hour and one fight later, surprised the door was still tightly locked as I passed through, I shoved it open again. They were just stripping his fighting togs off the ex-champion. Willie Ketchum and Eddie Foy III put fingers to their lips as they saw me. I closed the door softly. I thought the fighter was under sedation.

He was—God's sedation. A merciful curtain had been drawn over the awful pain the instant he said, "Ooh, my head hurts!" Davey Moore, for the first time in his career, was in a fight in which he was the underdog before it started. It was a fight in which the line wasn't posted by Vegas but on an invisible tote board with no wire service, only a chart at the foot of the bed.

There are excuses. There always are. Davey is a puncher. He always approached every fight as if his opponent were a punching bag. He worries about the other fellow's head and lets his own take care of itself. He fought Sugar Ramos as if the fellow owed him money. A ringsider pointed out it was not a fight, it was Russian roulette with 6-ounce gloves.

Davey had always been a lovely little fellow as merry as a spring day out of the ring. He had five kids named after movie stars and other minor celebrities. "My wife loves movies," he used to kid. He took a job parking cars at a Santa Monica hotel between fights and some wrote that this was undignified, as if honest work is ever undignified. Is dignity in fighters only bright lights and fast cars and fast girls? Moore had the great dignity of common sense. "He was cheap," the fight mob whispered. But maybe his kids didn't think so.

Born too small—and maybe too soon since the color of his face or any face won't matter as much and maybe not at all one hundred years from now—he could not be the football player he wanted to be, nor the baseball player. He

could only get out of his personal economic trap on horseback or in boxing gloves. He fought his way into an even
worse one. Is the fault Sugar Ramos'? His manager's? The
promoters'? No. It's ours.

I have fought on this prose level before. The counter has
been that people are killed in traffic, over water, under
ground. Sure, but we don't sell tickets.

Kids die in sandlot football, Little League baseball. But
these are champions, the highest practitioners of their art,
that we are admitting to hospitals, mausoleums and vege-
tation in boxing, not kids in unsupervised activity. Only
one big league baseball player, only one big league football
player has ever been killed. Even that is too many but no
match at all for boxing's toll. People die in auto racing. But
they kill themselves. And they are not trying to. As I said before, in boxing, it's the name of the game. "Kill him!" the
crowd cries. They boo at anything sub-lethal. They did
Thursday when Luis Rodriguez fought as sensibly as if he
had been put in the ring with a killer—precisely because he
was. Suicide is tragic but sanctioned murder is unconscion-
able.

My colleagues dispute me, ascribe cynical motives to my
periodic outcries. I understand that, too. Removal of any
sport diminishes our range for rhetoric. I'm willing to take
the chance. Better to lose readers than lives. Right is right
and boxing isn't. It has had more second chances than it
deserves.

Beauty and the Beast

It so happens that Gene Fullmer is the middleweight champion of the world and Ray Robinson merely the contender. But nobody in this wide-open town which makes its living taking the percentages seems to be taking it this time.

The crowds flock to Robinson's lavish training camp in the Dunes Hotel. They walk past Fullmer's to get to the crap tables. When the fighters hold a joint press conference, as they did Wednesday, it is at Robinson's quarters because they know Robinson won't show up if they don't. It is Gene who makes the trip.

When the question of color of trunks came up at the conference, it was Robinson who insisted on white even though that is the traditional color for the defending champ. Fullmer had to agree to a differentiating stripe down the side if he wanted white, too. Not that anybody will be confused which is which because no one confuses Robinson, the Sugar Man, the stylist, with Fullmer, the throwback. But Gene resents it. "Robinson," he says bitterly, "still thinks he's champ."

So, it appears, does the rest of the world. In its way, it's rather pathetic.

Gene Fullmer is a thoroughly nice, earnest young man who has paid dearly for his success in the ring with a lumpy face and scar tissue over both eyes after only fifty-eight fights. Robinson is a prettified dandy with few if any marks after 155 fights.

Gene did farm chores as a boy. Robinson ranged the

streets of Harlem with a gang and did things Gene
wouldn't even have known about at the time.

Where Robinson is a Lenox Avenue flash type who goes
through life leading a bank of clacking sycophants, Gene is
the kind of guy the stage magician calls out of the audience
to put funny hats on and pull jokes on and rabbits out of
his pocket.

Robinson's pulse is sixty-four. Gene's is forty-eight. Robinson is always on the qui vive. Gene is looking for a place
to go to sleep.

Robinson fights against authority from the low level of
boxing commissioners to the rarefied area of the U.S. Army
in wartime. Gene does what he's told.

Robinson drives a fuchsia Cadillac. Gene has a 1957 Mer-
cury Ed Sullivan gave him the only time he was on his TV
show. Robinson had been on more than the dog acts.

Robinson is not educated. He was dancing in the streets
for pennies when he should have been going to school. But
he has the quick intelligence and fast patter of the jazz
combo sideman. Gene thinks before he speaks and does
both slowly and thoroughly, grammatical but not witty.

Robinson flashes a smile constantly even when his eyes
don't. Gene is solemn and never mocking.

The "Grand Club," the well-heeled gambling bosses who
are paying $1000 to sit in a lounge chair at ringside, will be
paying to see Ray Robinson, not Fullmer. Robinson is the
Taj Mahal or Westminster Abbey of boxing, something to
see before you die if you are a fight man. Gene Fullmer is
the corner drug store. There's one in every block.

Robinson is a blithe spirit. He boasts he does everything
in life in rhythm, to the tune of some secret song that sets
his feet to moving. Gene might listen, but he can't hear a
thing. He can't even dance. Robinson is a man who back-

slaps the rich and famous shamelessly ("you're mah man, admiral . . ."). Gene speaks only when spoken to.

I took up this thesis with the comedian, Don Rickles, a midnight or so ago. He dug. "Fullmer," he elaborated, "is the kind of guy who would want to know what country Count Basie came from. Where Ray might invite Cab Calloway's band to the fight, Gene would ask the agricultural inspector from Ogden.

"When he was a kid, for kicks, Ray would ask a girl to dance. Gene would go up to his brother and say 'Let's rassle.' When Ray was stompin' at the Savoy, Gene was stompin' on crickets.

"If they ask Ray how he is going to fight Fullmer, he'll say 'with a cape.'"

And so it goes. Fullmer is the forgotten man who has affronted a nation's sense of what is right. It is a situation not unique in boxing. Gene Tunney, for whom Fullmer was named, defeated Jack Dempsey and schoolboys all over the country stuck pins in his picture through their tears. Rocky Marciano knocked out Joe Louis and no one spoke to him in Toots Shor's for months. They never forgave Sandy Saddler for beating Willie Pep.

If you have never seen the fighters, you will know which is Fullmer Saturday night. He'll be the one they're booing.

He won't admit it, but it hurts. He comforts himself by blaming it on his style.

"I couldn't look good fighting Robinson if I fought him 100 times," he admits.

It's too true. Even when he wins.

Stop, Look 'n Liston

The first look you get at Sonny Liston, you only hope it doesn't bite.

You get the idea Floyd Patterson shouldn't fight him, Clyde Beatty should. Patterson should bring a whip, a chair and a gun that shoots blanks in the ring. Or one that shoots bullets.

Liston would be an 8–5 favorite over the Marines. He already has beaten more cops than Perry Mason.

You go out to his training camp at an abandoned race track in Aurora and when he comes in you panic—because you think someone has forgotten to hold a rope around his neck. I never thought I would see anything like it when I was awake. And if I was asleep, I would wake up screaming. You half expect it to roar. Two people saw him doing road-work one morning and called the circus to see if any of their cages had been vacated.

If I were Patterson, I would make bloody sure Sonny had eaten before he went in the ring. If Liston gets hungry in the middle of the fight he may not even throw the bones away.

Someone has dug up an old part of the archives to find out that if a man is knocked out of the ring, he gets twenty seconds to get back. But from the look of Liston's hands, Floyd may need a cab to get back. Instead of knocking him for a loop, he may knock him in The Loop. If Liston knocked me out of the ring, I would be inclined to let it go at that. I wouldn't get back in the ring if they gave me a week. I would take a fast inventory and if I had all my vital parts I would go take in a show. The man has such a fantastically long reach he could jab Patterson from the second row of ringside. He may score a few jabs from his stool.

The prevailing opinion in Chicago is Liston may knock out Patterson in 2m. and 9s. of the introduction. They brought a hypnotist into the camps, presumably to hypnotize the champion against pain. But when the hypnotist got a look at Liston, they had to revive him.

The late Arthur Brisbane, a journalist, used to boast that a gorilla could lick any fighter but up to now I never thought we'd live to see it done. Sonny Liston is such an awesome specimen that even though you know he can't read or write, the big shock is that he talks.

His fist is so huge his boxing gloves look like saddles. Patterson's manager is holding out for a brand of gloves he knows won't even keep Sonny's hands warm. He should throw in a pair of handcuffs.

The betting around town among people who saw Liston is not whether Patterson will win or lose but whether he will show up. There are those who think Sonny can knock him out even if he doesn't.

Liston's camp is a light-hearted place—for everybody but the sparring partners. When they go home in single file they look like the retreat at Dunkirk. Sonny broke Big Jim Robinson's ribs. If he ever hit him on the head he'd henceforth be known as "Little Jim Robinson." Lou Bailey tried a couple of rounds and left the ring, the camp and ultimately the state. He complained his head still hurt two weeks later —but those who saw the workout say he was lucky he had one left to hurt.

They're allowed to take pain pills, but morphine would be more humane. In fact, the best guess is that the hypnotist was really going to work on the sparring partners. Sonny ran out of them so fast he would have had to take his workouts to the Chicago Zoo to find opponents. But the Society for Prevention of Cruelty to Animals would have stalled that.

His chest, neck, fist, thigh, wrist and calf are all 1 to 4 in. bigger than Patterson's. If you saw his footprint in the snow in the Himalayas, four expeditions would be launched to capture him. As long as he lives, man can believe in the Abominable Snowman.

He has been celebrated in print as one of the few guys who ever could think of anything to do in Philadelphia after dark. He chased a woman off the highway with a red light and fast car and was surprised she didn't know he was joking.

He is the best argument I know for schooling. He never had any and if he wins he's going to be stuck with all those millions of dollars and not even know which salad fork to use. Tunney read Shakespeare, but Sonny has a tough time with a No Smoking sign.

He is so sure he is going to be champion that his only fear is Patterson will get hit by a streetcar before the fight. He got his jaw broken by a fighter named Marty Marshall one night because he was laughing at Marshall. "I never laughed in the ring since," he explains. He might add he seldom does out of it, either. "They say I look evil and mean. If you got your jaw broke you'd look the way I look," he told me.

Patterson's speed bores him. "We ain't gonna race," he explains. He is of the opinion the only way Patterson can survive the fifth round is by hiding under the ring until the sixth.

Archie's Secret

A droll fellow, Archie Moore. You not only get fifteen rounds of impeccable box-fighting out of him, you also get a controlled filibuster at the end of the merits of a milk diet drink, your friendly corner diamond store, the Ancient Order of Hibernians, the Salvation Army—or whatever other enthusiasm Archie has at the moment. He has more commercials than the Late, Late Show and even Gillette used to be hard put to get a draw when Archie was on camera.

It has been suggested that Archie's ring costume makes him look like a guy that just got out of a hotel fire in time but I have always figured Archie wanted the pants that long in case he had a product with a long name to advertise down the side some night—in neon.

The best description I ever heard of Archie's ring style was one Mel Durslag gave me once when he said, "Archie is the best mechanic who ever stepped in a ring."

It's true. Even today, watching Archie climb through the ropes, it is possible to picture him as a guy who has come to fix the plumbing or flush the carburetor. He seems, figuratively, to drop his box of tools in a corner and wander over to check the problem at hand to see whether it calls for a Stilson wrench, a pair of pliers or just a simple kick on the side of the set.

The early rounds of a Moore fight always remind me of a guy opening the hood of an engine and exploring around inside for weak spots. Only, when he finds them, he doesn't repair them. He makes them worse. It's a trick a lot of mechanics have but with Dr. Moore it's a high art. A loose bolt here, a sticky valve there and by the time Arch has gotten through tinkering, the transmission falls out. Even those long drawers get to look like a pair of coveralls Laurel and Hardy might get tangled up in while trying to fix a leak in the bathtub.

In a way, Archie Moore is an affront to the society in which you and I live. I mean, here he is in the ring whomping the daylights out of a trained young athlete half his age while the rest of us shrink from telling a bunch of teen-aged punks accosting girls on the beach to knock it off.

And because I have genuine admiration for him, it pains me somewhat to have to remind myself that in some respects our Arch is a lovable old fraud.

Archie, you see, achieved his unique place in the game not by being better than his counterparts but by lasting longer. Archie came up just as the fight game was going down. One-by-one, better fighters dropped by the wayside— gin, girls, gullibility—each found his downfall. Suddenly, Archie found himself virtually alone—except for a pack of clumsy Europeans, a gym-ful of half-schooled kids, a strong-backed Canadian fisherman, a fragile kid from Harlem with a glass chin. Archie was like a kid who inherits a candy store. He couldn't believe his luck after all those hungry years.

Even at that, Archie has to pick his spots carefully. Every really good fighter he fights knocks him out. It has always been that way. Archie has tried to convey the impression that he has historically been the Satchel Paige of the prize ring—the man the champions ducked or ignored. It is not altogether true. Ezzard Charles fought Archie every time anyone was interested enough to come see it—and beat him all three times. The last time he knocked him out. Archie couldn't even catch Jack Chase, the California middleweight phantom, until Jack had lost his speed.

A nobody named Eddie Booker knocked Archie kicking. Jimmy Bivins flattened him. Archie, in short, had his troubles in his prime. It is only now that he is past his prime that the competition has evaporated. There is an Oriental proverb which holds that a man's youth does not die unless he kills it. Archie took excellent care of Archie's youth, and will nurse it into his old age, if that ever comes.

Archie has had over two hundred fights. He has scored, by his own count, over 130 kayos. But nobody ever beat as many *unknown* fighters as Archie Moore. Names like Herman Harris, Esco Greenwood, Victor Carabajal and Sterling Davis dot his record book. Giulio Rinaldi and Yvon Durelle are, on class, unknown fighters. They are known only because they fought Ancient Arch.

The last good fighters Archie fought knocked him out— Patterson and Marciano. He has not fought Harold Johnson since 1954, arguing there's no point in it. For Archie, there sure isn't. Archie kayoed Johnson in fourteen that year but he owed the fact he was around till the fourteenth to the fact that when Johnson knocked him down in the tenth, the referee began a mandatory 8-count which is illegal in title fights. The bell saved Moore because Referee Goldstein was holding off Johnson while he counted to eight.

The Old Fellows

Jimmy Jacobs of Brentwood is probably the world's greatest handball player, several times national champ, and, if he'll take my advice, he'll let it go at that.

But Jimmy is a man enmeshed in his first crusade. And it's hard on him.

Jimmy has set out on the thankless task of destroying people's illusions for them, an activity I don't recommend to anybody. Jimmy, it so happens, thinks the old-time fighters were a bunch of bums and he has gone to considerable expense to prove it.

He has a collection of old fight films and he will whip them out like a set of French postcards at the slightest provocation. Jimmy seems to think they show conclusively that Joe Louis could whip Jack Johnson, Rocky Graziano could take Stanley Ketchel and Lee Oma could probably chase Bob Fitzsimmons right out of the ring.

I would have liked to duck this one if I could. But Jimmy would have none of it. Personally, I wouldn't spend 40 cents to prove Jim Corbett couldn't get out of the way of a right hand with a bicycle. And I would rather see the late, late show than Johnson and Ketchel. But Jimmy has spent so much money on these films that Lloyd's of London would be in trouble if he so much as cancelled the insurance on them. He has to show them.

Old-time fight fans have taken to ducking when they see Jimmy coming. They know all they have to do is murmur "Jim Jeffries was the greatest of them all . . ." and pretty soon Jimmy will be hip-deep in film negatives and shouting, "I just happen to have the movies right here which show he wasn't a patch on Ezzard Charles. If you have a minute . . ."

Poor Old Nat Fleischer of *Ring Magazine* is a particular target of Jim's, who cannot understand how Nat maintains his position as the Boswell of Boxing when all the time he thinks Jack Johnson or Jim Corbett could handle Joe Louis or Jack Dempsey.

Prior to Jacobs, Nat got away for years with the propaganda that the old-timers were best. If he had been fast enough to keep Jimmy out of the archives of the Library of Congress, he might still get away with it.

Jimmy took Rocky Marciano, me and a crew of other bewildered characters up to the actor Scott Brady's house the other afternoon to give us the latest scoop on Corbett and Fitzsimmons, Johnson and Jeffries, et al.

I have to admit some of it was high comedy. Jimmy's most devastating piece of evidence is a staged fight in Edison's kinescope laboratory between Corbett and an Englishman named Peter Courtney.

This Courtney was really something. I only wish my wife were that clumsy in a fight. He fought like he was trying to run up the side of a greased tree. He didn't punch. He just held his arms straight out and ran into the other guy. Corbett didn't look too good, either. He was laughing too hard.

In the Fitzsimmons-Corbett title fight, poor old Fitz with his bald head showed up in a long overcoat looking for all the world like a guy who had just come downstairs with a cake of soap and a towel over his arm to get in line in the boarding-house shower. He fought like a stork with a backache.

"They look like dopes," exclaimed Scott Brady. "I cahn't believe it," murmured Rocky Marciano politely.

On the other hand, the films were jerky and inconclusive. And something did knock Jim Corbett kicking. He tried to get up and his feet splattered out from underneath him as though he had been lassoed.

There was one old character on hand, 83-year-old Bob Perry, who claimed to have seen all the old-timers and he was triumphant. "Fitz could punch as hard or harder than any man in the world," he announced defiantly.

Jacobs just looked reproachful. I don't really know what his films prove, though, except that the state of the art of prizefighting was in a primitive stage in those days. So, for that matter, was the art of the motion picture. Between the two, I doubt they did justice to the old fellows.

There is a confusion of communication between the two eras. For instance, Ketchel and Johnson were shown in a desultory Mutt and Jeff comedy. Suddenly, Ketchel floored Johnson. A new Johnson arose from the floor, fast and furious as a snake. He lashed out and put an end to the fight with such a shattering right Ketchel went down as though pole-axed, so hard and fast Johnson tripped over him. When Johnson got up, he blew one of Ketchel's teeth off his mitt and stood there glowering. In that one instant, you realized with a chill that these, too, were powerful, mighty men in those days.

I wish Jimmy luck. But I wish, too, he would remember a left jab is commonplace today. It wasn't when Corbett or whoever first thought it up. Boxing has progressed technically and movie technicians have improved on Edison. The point is, *he* did it when it was hard. So, maybe, did they.

It doesn't matter anyway. As we stumbled out into the sunlight, Bob Perry was still unreconstructed and, even after Jacobs' devastating proof to the contrary, insisted loudly, "I still say Jim Jeffries was the greatest of them all . . ."